About the Author

 Richard Southall (West Virginia) has been interested in the paranormal since a very young age and was conducting his own paranormal investigations by the time he was a teenager. He is the co-creator of a haunted walking tour of Parkersburg, WV, one of the best-received tours in the United States. Today, Southall conducts private ghost investigations, teaches workshops on ghost hunting, contributes to numerous periodicals, and has been interviewed on regional and national radio about ghosts and hauntings. He is a member of the paranormal group MAJDA.

To Write to the Author

If you wish to contact the author or would like more information about this book, please write to the author in care of Llewellyn Worldwide, and we will forward your request. Both the author and the publisher appreciate hearing from you and learning of your enjoyment of this book and how it has helped you. Llewellyn Worldwide cannot guarantee that every letter written to the author can be answered, but all will be forwarded. Please write to:

Richard Southall
⸮ Llewellyn Worldwide
2143 Wooddale Drive
Woodbury, MN 55125-2989

Please enclose a self-addressed stamped envelope for reply,
or $1.00 to cover costs. If outside the USA, enclose
an international postal reply coupon.

Many of Llewellyn's authors have websites with additional information and resources. For more information, please visit our website at: www .llewellyn.com.

RICHARD SOUTHALL

HAUNTED

ROUTE 66

GHOSTS OF AMERICA'S LEGENDARY HIGHWAY

Llewellyn Worldwide
Woodbury, Minnesota

FIRST EDITION
First Printing, 2013

Author photo © Debra Southall
Book design by Bob Gaul
Editing by Ed Day
Cover art: Clouds © iStockphoto.com/Milorad Zaric
          Interstate sign © iStockphoto.com/trekandshoot
          Storm, bird, road in desert © iStockphoto.com/Dmitry Rukhlenko/
          Woman © iStockphoto.com/Erik Khalitov
Cover design by Kevin R. Brown
Interior illustrations © Art Explosion and Llewellyn art department
Interior photos © Library of Congress, Barbara Schepker, Nancy Longhurst
          and Josh Millstein

Llewellyn Publications is a registered trademark of Llewellyn Worldwide Ltd.

Library of Congress Cataloging-in-Publication Data
Southall, Richard, 1972–
  Haunted Route 66: ghosts of America's legendary highway.—1st ed.
      p. cm.
  Includes bibliographical references and index.
  ISBN 978-0-7387-2636-6 (alk. paper)
  1. Ghosts—United States. 2. Haunted places—United States. 3. United States
Highway 66—Miscellanea. I. Title.
  BF1472.U6S675 2013
  133.10973—dc23
                          2012028545

Llewellyn Publications
A Division of Llewellyn Worldwide Ltd.
2143 Wooddale Drive
Woodbury, MN 55125-2989
www.llewellyn.com

Printed in the United States of America

Contents

(image courtesy Library of Congress)

Introduction

T he Mother Road. Main Street USA. Although it has been known by many names over the years, Route 66 has allowed us to embrace the spirit of adventure and freedom that is the epitome of our American heritage. Route 66 has been the inspiration behind books, music, television series, and movies for nearly a century. With such a vast history, Route 66 undoubtedly has its fair share of ghost stories. That is the purpose of this book ... to chronicle several of these accounts that have been passed down over the years. However, before we can journey down this road together, it is important to get some background of how Route 66 came into being.

History of Route 66

There are already several books published that can offer a more detailed and concise history of Route 66, so rather than provide yet another exhaustive account of the origins, near demise, and resurrection of Route 66, I will simply review the basics. If you want more in-depth historical information, I personally found that Drew Knowles's *Route 66 Adventure Handbook* was very helpful and could be used in conjunction with this book in order to get a feel for what the Mother Road has to offer.

Route 66 consisted of nearly 2,500 miles of road stretching from Chicago, Illinois, to Santa Monica, California. It goes through eight states: Illinois, Missouri, Kansas, Oklahoma, Texas, New Mexico, Arizona, and California. In the early 1920s, cars were being produced en masse and people started to buy them at an astounding rate. To meet the need, the United States government created a federal numbered highway system that linked existing roads together into an interstate route for people to travel. By the way, the official birthdate for Route 66 was November 11, 1926.

Route 66 was not actually one long roadway that started in Chicago and ended in Santa Monica, but rather a series of dozens of different roads that went through a multitude of towns between Illinois and California. These roads had existed long before Route 66 was commissioned. Rather than create a whole new road system, it was decided that the existing roads could be connected to form one continuous roadway from Illinois to California. Route 66 often led people into the downtowns of these communities. This is why Route 66 is often called Main Street USA—sometimes Route 66 actually was Main Street.

Residents of these towns began to notice the increase in traffic and visitors after Route 66 was commissioned. Literally hundreds of new businesses emerged to meet the increased demand of travelers. Restaurants, curio shops, roadside attractions, hotels, and other types of businesses began to sprout almost overnight. No two stops were the same. Many tried to be as unique as possible in order to stand out. It has been said that a person could travel Route 66 a hundred times and never have the same experience twice.

In its heyday, Route 66 was one of the finest examples of Americana and took on a life of its own in the 1940s and 1950s. People would take weeks to travel the route, always looking for adventure around every turn. The people who lived along and traveled on the 2,448 miles of highway from Chicago to Santa Monica were given an opportunity to express their individuality. New people, new attractions, and new stories were found along every mile of Main Street USA.

In the late 1950s, the federal government commissioned a new series of interstate highways that were designed to considerably cut the drive time for a motorist. The rationale was that with an interstate system, people and cargo could travel cross-country more efficiently. With fewer stops and longer stretches of highway, people could drive farther in a shorter amount of time.

Initially, several business owners in towns along Route 66 thought that the new interstate system would mean even more visitors and more business. In many cases, this new interstate system was constructed parallel to the original roads of Route 66. However, to save money, many of the towns were bypassed. Being cut off from the increasing flow of the interstate traffic, businesses and entire communities suffered. One by one, businesses closed and some of the towns were entirely abandoned, simply fading into history. Eventually, a great piece of Americana was lost. Officially, Route 66 was decommissioned on June 27, 1985. You will not find any official reference to Route 66 on a roadmap printed after 1985. In recent years, several road signs have been erected to commemorate the original route of "Historic Route 66."

Our Changing Societal Mindset

The decommissioning of Route 66 was a harbinger of change. A look at the interstate system that replaced the Mother Road is a telltale sign that since the 1980s, we have been in the process of transitioning from a society of quality to a society of quantity. We simply want to get from Point A to Point B in the fastest, most efficient way possible.

What has happened with Route 66 also appears to be happening in other parts of our lives. More and more people would prefer to interact with each other via Facebook than in real life. Some would rather play Farmville than attempt to grow a real garden. We tend to overlook the important things in our lives as we hurry from appointment to appointment. As technology continues to advance, we are slowly losing our connection to others and to our history. There is an uncanny parallel between what the interstate system did to Route 66 and what technology is doing to our society.

If we are not careful, we could lose that spirit of adventure that America was founded upon and exchange it for one of convenience and comfort. This goes against everything that Route 66 stood for. Perhaps it was the great Charlie Chaplin that said it best in the final scene from his controversial film, *The Great Dictator*.

> *We have developed speed but we have shut ourselves in:*
> *machinery that gives abundance has left us in want.*
> *Our knowledge has made us cynical,*
> *our cleverness hard and unkind.*
> *We think too much and feel too little:*
> *More than machinery we need humanity;*
> *More than cleverness we need kindness and gentleness.*
> *Without these qualities, life will be violent and all will be lost.*

Although these words were said over seven decades ago, they still ring as true today as when they were so enthusiastically spoken by Chaplin. Although he was talking about the condition of life during World War II, he just as easily could have been referring to the early twenty-first century and the way that technology has both brought us closer together while it has made us more distant than ever.

Still, there are people who recognize the importance of reconnecting to the spirit of adventure that made the Mother Road so amazing. Although there are several locations throughout the United States where people can get in touch with their past, Route 66 is like no other. It represents a time long before commercialized fast food restaurants, convenience stores, and Wal-Marts; part of the wonder of driving Route 66 is the journey, not necessarily the destination. The Mother Road has become a time capsule that invites us to re-experience a slower, more deliberate time that many of us long for as we race along at a breakneck pace toward an uncertain future.

Why Ghost Stories?

Why write a book of ghost stories that take place along Route 66? For several reasons. First, ghost stories have a way of uniting us. No matter what our differences are, most people like to hear about others' experiences with things that go bump in the night. Sharing ghost stories with each other helps to preserve our past. Granted, some of the stories in this book are actually urban legends, which can be just as important as true ghostly experiences. At some point in a town's past, a real event occurred (car accident, suicide, murder, etc.) and word got out. Over time, these stories get told and retold to the point that there is little resemblance between the actual event and the story. To make the story more interesting, whispers of paranormal events are often added. And, thus, an urban legend is born.

Second, we want to believe. Whether it's experiencing a ghost recording in an abandoned asylum while on a ghost tour or being reassured by a personal message from a loved one who has recently passed, we want to believe that there is more to our reality than our day-to-day existence of forty-hour workweeks and paying bills.

Third, we like to be scared. This would explain the recent revival in paranormal topics in books (The *Twilight* Saga, *Abraham Lincoln: Vampire Hunter*), television shows (*Ghost Adventures, True Blood, Paranormal State*, etc.), video games (Resident Evil, FEAR, etc.) and movies (*Paranormal Activity, The Devil Inside*, etc.). We simply cannot get enough of the paranormal. Although we know the movies and television shows are fiction, we realize that many of the stories we hear from others may have some truth to them. With paranormal groups and ghost tours sprouting up in every state across the nation, it is now cool to belong to a ghost hunting group and go to a place with the intention of being frightened.

I decided to write this book on the paranormal events of Route 66 because with the richness of the Mother Road, there undoubtedly would be several stories that will unite us, cause us to believe in the unseen, and scare us. The legends and stories from the towns along Route 66, and of any community for that matter, often serve as reminders of actual events in the town's past. These stories tell of how local landmarks got their names. They immortalize key people and events that helped to mold a town into what it is today. These stories allow the towns to have a historical significance and individuality that is the epitome of everything that Route 66 stands for. This book is being written partially to make certain that the tradition of storytelling is continued and can be shared for many years to come.

Do people experience the paranormal in their lives? Every day. Over the years, do some of these experiences evolve into the urban legends and folktales that are passed down from generation to generation? Absolutely. It is up to the reader to determine the difference between the two.

Several of the stories in this book go back to a time prior to Route 66's construction. I would like to think that this is more than simply a book of ghost stories. For those who want to travel Main Street USA or live near many of the cities and attractions listed here, I would like to think of this as a guidebook that will whet your appetite to seek to experience the paranormal firsthand.

Although I acknowledge that some of these accounts are stories that have been told and retold to the point that they may have very little resemblance to the actual facts, I also have to acknowledge that some of these stories are in fact real. Average people have had paranormal or supernatural experiences happen to them for hundreds of years. Some people do not share their experiences with others for fear of ridicule. However, others are brave enough to share their experiences with others...their stories should be heard.

Are the ghost stories in this book tales of a real haunting or the product by creative minds? I will leave that question for you to answer on your own. But for now, sit back, relax, and prepare to be entertained by the many ghost stories that have sprung up over the years along Route 66.

ONE

ILLINOIS

---

301 miles

Some of our country's most significant events have taken place in Illinois. The Great Chicago Fire. Al Capone and the St. Valentine's Day Massacre. John Dillinger being gunned down at the Biograph Theater. The Eastland Ship Disaster that claimed several hundred lives one fateful morning. The list goes on.

With such a wide brushstroke of American culture ranging from mafia kingpins to talk show gurus, Illinois's history is filled with some of the most unique and colorful historical figures of any state. Because of this, it may seem fitting that we begin our journey of Haunted Route 66 in Chicago, Illinois.

Chicago

· · · · · · · · · · · · · · · ·

The Great Chicago Fire of 1871

Any history of Chicago would not be complete without a discussion of the Great Chicago Fire of 1871. The

9

Great Chicago Fire started around 9:00 p.m., Sunday, October 8, 1871, and finally burned itself out two days later on October 10. The official story is that the fire started in a barn owned by Patrick and Catherine O'Leary, who owned a farm at 137 DeKoven Street. It is popularly believed that Mrs. O'Leary's cow kicked over a lantern, which ignited a pile of hay. However, it was determined that the "Mrs. O'Leary's Cow" theory was actually fabricated by Michael Ahern, reporter for the *Chicago Republican*, because it was a "more colorful story." He finally admitted to creating the story of Mrs. O'Leary's cow in 1893. Although the O'Leary account was determined to be a fabrication, there are at least two lesser-known hypotheses that are just as likely to explain the cause of the fire.

The first hypothesis does in fact involve the O'Leary's cow. The story goes that Daniel "Pegleg" Sullivan may have accidently started the Great Chicago Fire when he was trying to steal milk from O'Leary's cow and placed his lantern too close to a pile of hay. Before he could do anything, a fire started and quickly consumed the barn. Sullivan ran away, fearful that he would get in trouble for trespassing.

A second hypothesis is that the Great Chicago Fire was caused when Biela's Comet broke up over the Midwest and that the fragments fell to the ground. This theory was first presented by physicist Robert Wood at the 2004 Aerospace Corporation and the American Institute of Aeronautics and Astronautics. Wood attests that there were reports of at least three other devastating fires that took place near Lake Michigan that day. Several eyewitnesses noted that "balls of fire" were seen falling from the sky shortly before the fires were first reported.

One fire completely destroyed Peshtigo, Wisconsin, and surrounding communities. A second fire, known as the Great Michigan Fire, also destroyed most of Manistee, Michigan. The Port Huron Fire, which consumed much of Port Huron, also took place on Sunday, October 8, 1871. Although some of these fires were actually more destructive in terms of loss of life and burnt acreage, the Great Chicago Fire is likely the most renowned because Chicago had the largest population.

Whatever the cause of the Great Chicago Fire, we know that it was destructive. Over 2,000 acres and nearly 18,000 buildings were destroyed in the fire. About one-third of the city's 300,000 people were left homeless. There were approximately 300 people who died in the fire. Of that number, only 125 bodies were recovered. Needless to say, with numbers like this there are bound to be several ghost stories associated with the Great Chicago Fire... and ghost stories there are.

Water Tower of Chicago
806 North Michigan Avenue

The Water Tower of Chicago on North Michigan Avenue was one of the few structures that survived the Great Chicago Fire. According to local legend, the Water Tower is haunted by the ghost of a firefighter who gave his life for his city. Apparently, the fireman on duty pumped water as it continued to consume the wooden buildings surrounding the tower. He was so focused on saving the other buildings that he did not notice the fire starting to surround him in the water tower. When he realized that he would not be able to stop the fire and was going to be burned alive, the fireman reportedly hung himself from near the top of the tower. To this day, his ghost has been seen hanging from one of the windows in the upper part of the water tower.

Hull House/Jane Addams Hull House
800 South Halstead Street

The mansion that eventually became known as Hull House was built in 1856 by Charles Hull, a well-known man who had made his fortune in the real estate industry. When it was built by Hull, the area was one of the most upscale and prominent in Chicago. However, when Jane Addams was looking for a location to provide services to immigrants, the area had deteriorated into one of Chicago's poorest neighborhoods. By this time,

Hull was no longer living in the home and gave his niece the property. She was so impressed with Addams's vision that she let her have it with a twenty-five-year lease.

Hull House was founded in 1889 by Ellen Gates Starr and Jane Addams. The primary purpose of Hull House was to help European immigrants make the transition to living in the United States. It provided immigrants and local citizens with a variety of educational programs (literature, theater, history, etc.) and social opportunities that they probably would not receive otherwise. Hull House also provided free lectures and concerts that were open to the public. There were a variety of clubs available for adults and children. In addition, volunteers and staff members became vocal against some of the social wrongs of the day... child labor, homelessness, women's rights, discrimination against immigrants, and the like. Some historians claim that the variety of services that Hull House was one of the first examples of organized social welfare in the United States.

By the time Addams moved into the original mansion, it had already become known as a haunted hotspot. Hull's wife had died after a long illness in 1860, only four years after the mansion had been constructed. People have claimed to see an image of a woman that looked like Mrs. Hull looking out a bedroom window even after Mr. Hull decided to move. Addams has been quoted as saying to friends and volunteers at Hull House that a woman wearing white could sometimes be seen looking out one of the bedrooms on the second floor, which was reportedly the same room where Mrs. Hull had died. Other ghosts were likely to be those of people who had died in the 1870s prior to Addams's moving in and a few people who had died of natural causes while residing at Hull House.

S-M-C Cartage Company
2122 Clark Street

Al "Scarface" Capone (1899–1947) made his fortune bootlegging liquor during Prohibition (1919–1933) and through other illegal activities (gambling, prostitution, bribery of elected officials, etc.) from the early 1920s until his arrest for tax evasion in 1931. Capone had been involved with gang activity since he was a teenager living in Brooklyn, New York. In 1918, Capone moved to Chicago at the request of Johnny Torrio, a fellow gang member who needed some help taking care of some "family business." Financially, it was a sound decision for Capone, who had a young wife and newborn son to take care of. Although he amassed a great deal of wealth through his illegal endeavors, Capone was also known as a philanthropist. He was hated by authorities and loved by the masses, often being called a modern-day Robin Hood. He was often quoted as saying that he was just a businessman who was providing the people of Chicago what they wanted.

Of particular interest to Capone was the rivalry that had started between his organization, the South Side Italian Outfit, and the North Side Gang. In May 1924, Dean O'Banion of the North Side Gang agreed to sell a brewery to Johnny Torrio, the leader of Capone's gang. O'Banion knew that there was going to be a raid on the brewery and wanted it out of his hands, so he sold it to Torrio at a low price. During the raid, O'Banion and Torrio were both arrested. In an act of revenge, O'Banion was found murdered on October 10, 1924, at his flower shop on North State Street. In retaliation of O'Banion's murder, there was a 1925 assassination attempt against Torrio, who was severely injured. Johnny Torrio returned to Italy and put Capone in charge. At the age of twenty-six, Al Capone found himself in the middle of a gang war that spread through the city of Chicago for several years.

After O'Banion's death, there were several men who attempted to take control of the North Side Gang, but each person was eventually taken down. Finally, George "Bugs" Moran assumed control of the North Side Gang, which rose in power to rival Capone's gang. The gang war continued for nearly five years, eventually leading to the Saint Valentine's Day Massacre.

On the morning of Thursday, February 14, 1929, four armed men (two dressed as police officers) went to the S-M-C Cartage Company building in search of Bugs Moran. The men were unable to find Moran, but did find five high-ranking members of the North Side Gang, a hired auto mechanic, and a man who had retired from gang life and had simply been visiting his friends. The seven men were lined up against a brick wall inside the company and were summarily executed. The murder weapons were two Thompson submachine guns (tommy guns), followed by two shotgun blasts at close range into the faces of two of the victims. Each of the men had been hit by between twelve and twenty-five bullets. Frank Gusenberg was the only man still living when the police finally arrived, although he had been hit by fourteen bullets. He was taken to a nearby hospital and after he was somewhat stabilized, he was asked who had shot him. His reply? "Nobody shot me."

The garage where the St. Valentine's Day Massacre took place was demolished in 1967 to make way for the parking lot of a nursing home that still stands today. To this day, people claim to hear the sound of machine-gun fire followed by screams. Sometimes the sounds are accompanied by the smell of blood and an overpowering sense of dread.

When the actual wall was dismantled, it went up for auction. Canadian businessman George Patey outbid two or three other men to purchase the bricks. He had numbered each of the 414 bricks and had them shipped back to Canada. Over the years, the bricks were on display in a wax museum, placed in a bar, and nearly one hundred had been individually sold online. When Patey died, he left the remaining bricks to his niece, who ended up selling them to the Las Vegas Mob Museum. According to legend, there is a curse associated with the bricks. Anybody who possesses a brick for any length of time will suffer sickness, financial loss, horrible luck, and a terrible death.

Biograph Theater
2433 North Lincoln Avenue

John Dillinger was a career criminal who made a living from robbing banks. Dillinger and his gang robbed at least two dozen banks, although some experts believe that the number was actually closer to thirty bank robberies. In addition to robbing banks, the gang robbed at least four police stations of uniforms, weapons, and bulletproof vests. Dillinger had become such a "menace to society" that J. Edgar Hoover would use Dillinger's gang and their criminal activities as catalyst to launch the newly formed Federal Bureau of Investigation.

However, as fascinating as Dillinger's exploits were, our interest in Dillinger focuses not on his life of crime, but rather his death and subsequent haunting of a historical theater in downtown Chicago. Dillinger had successfully escaped capture for over a year while continuing to rob banks in four states, including Indiana and Ohio.

Finally, federal agents were contacted by Ana Cumpanas (aka Anna Sage) on July 21,1934. She was a madam at a Gary, Indiana, brothel that Dillinger was known to frequent. She was an illegal immigrant from Romania who had recently been threatened with deportation. Cumpanas agreed to lead authorities to Dillinger in exchange for taking care of her deportation problem. Since there were no other solid leads on Dillinger's whereabouts, authorities agreed to her terms. Cumpanas said that Dillinger was spending time with a woman named Polly Hamilton, one of her prostitutes that Dillinger had taken a liking to. Cumpanas told authorities that she, Polly Hamilton, and John Dillinger would be going to a movie the next day. To help federal agents identify the trio, Cumpanas agreed to wear a red dress to the movie. Although she was uncertain of the exact time and place, she knew it was going to be either the Biograph Theater on Chicago's North Side or the Marbo Theater on Chicago's West Side.

The following day, July 22, 1934, federal agents and police officers from jurisdictions outside of Chicago (there was concern that Dillinger had informants on the Chicago Police Department) staked out both the Marbo and Biograph Theaters.

Dillinger went to see a performance of the MGM film *Manhattan Melodrama* with Hamilton and Cumpanas. As promised, she wore a red dress, and they were easy to spot in the crowd.

After the show, Dillinger realized that there were federal agents and authorities waiting for him. He attempted to reach his gun as he ran into the alley beside the theater. Three agents were waiting for him and fired five shots. Three of the bullets hit Dillinger from behind. Two of the bullets pierced his chest and the third entered his neck and exited below his right eye. Based on the severity of his wounds, it was apparent that he died quickly. When bystanders realized who had been shot, some approached the body and dipped their handkerchiefs in the expanding pool of blood as a souvenir. Although it was obvious that Dillinger was dead, his body was taken to Alexian Brothers Hospital where he was pronounced dead at 10:28 p.m. Ironically, although Dillinger had robbed banks of over $300,000 in 1933 and 1934, he only had $7.81 in his pocket when he was killed.

In the years since Dillinger's death, there have been hundreds of sightings of a man running down the alleyway only to suddenly fall and disappear in the exact spot where Dillinger was ambushed. People have also heard the sounds of a person running followed by five distinct gunshots. Most believe that it is the ghost of Dillinger himself replaying the final moments of his life.

Red Lion Pub
2446 North Lincoln Avenue

Directly across the street from the Biograph Theater is the Red Lion Pub. It was an English pub built in 1882 and was a popular part of the Chicago nightlife for several decades before Dillinger's death at the Biograph Theater. Over the years, the Red Lion Pub developed a reputation for being haunted by the ghosts of past regular patrons and bartenders. On more than one occasion, patrons have ordered drinks from a bartender, only to find that there was nobody working that fit that description. Most of the paranormal activity at the Red Lion Pub was not visual, but rather auditory. Usually, patrons and staff experienced the sound of voices, running footsteps, the sound of glass breaking, and piano music playing. In addition, doors were seen opening and closing by themselves and bottles of liquor were found to have been rearranged on the shelves of behind the bar. Based on this type of activity, it is likely that one of the ghosts at the Red Lion Pub is that of a bartender or other employee that died long ago. Unfortunately, a few years ago the Red Lion Pub closed its doors after nearly 130 years of operation.

The Eastland Ship Disaster
Chicago River

The Eastland Ship Disaster (image courtesy Library of Congress)

The Eastland Ship Disaster took place on the morning of July 24, 1915. The Eastland had been commissioned by Western Electric for a sightseeing excursion and picnic on the Chicago River for employees and their families. By 7:00 a.m., there were over 2,700 people crowded onto the Eastland. While the ship was tied to the dock between LaSalle and Clark Streets, too many people went to the port side of the ship to watch other boats along the river before their departure, which made the ship go off balance and capsize. This in turn caused the ship to quickly start sinking with nearly 3,000 people still on board, many of whom were below deck. When the ship sank, a total of 849 people (including four crew members) died in the single worst ship accident in terms of loss of life recorded in Chicago's history. Several bystanders could hear the screams of the men, women, and children trapped below deck grow in volume before fading into an eerie silence as they all drowned within a few minutes, less than twenty feet from shore.

Soon after the ship sank came the grim task of recovering the bodies. Many who died included women and children who were trapped below deck. Mothers had taken their young children to the heated lower deck in order to break the chill of the early morning air. Due to the sheer number of bodies recovered, at least two nearby office buildings were converted into makeshift morgues.

The first building where the bodies of the Eastland victims were taken to was the Second Regimental Armory on North Carpenter Street. It had a refrigerated warehouse on site where hundreds of bodies were placed for easy identification and collection. This was a blessing because the refrigeration helped preserve the bodies so that they could be identified and collected by grieving family members.

Nearly sixty years after the Eastland Ship Disaster, the renovated building became the home office of Harpo Studios, the central hub of the recently canceled *Oprah Winfrey Show* and now the Oprah Winfrey Network.

There have been many reports of paranormal activity in the office building for several years. Dozens of employees and visitors to Harpo Studios have claimed to hear children's laughter, women's sobs and screams, and the sound of broken glass. There have also been several who claim to hear 1920s popular music played throughout different parts of the building.

A second building converted into an impromptu morgue was the Former Historical Society Building, built in 1892 and located at 632 North Dearborn. It is known by locals as the Excalibur Club or simply Excalibur because there is currently a nightclub by that name residing on the site. At least three spirits associated with the Eastland disaster haunt the Excalibur Club. The first ghost is that of a woman in her early forties wearing a red dress. She has been described as an attractive woman, but also appears to be somewhat confused, as if she is lost. Another ghost on the first floor is an older, distinguished bearded man wearing a white suit or tuxedo. Finally, there have been reports of a little girl seen running along the first floor. The little girl is not running in fear; she appears to be playing. She is usually seen on the first floor for only a few seconds before she disappears. All of these ghosts have been reported on the first floor where the bodies were placed for identification by authorities and family members. In addition to the apparitions, employees and people who come to the Excalibur also claim to hear breaking glass in the bar area as well as crying from a downstairs bathroom.

It is interesting to note that both places that were used as morgues report sounds of breaking glass. The sound could either be from the breaking glass of the Eastland as it capsized or from people attempting to break windows in a frantic effort to escape drowning.

If you would happen to walk across or near the Clark Street Bridge, there is a good chance that you could hear the screams of the dying passengers from the Eastland. Ironically, the Clark Street Bridge is on the same street where the St. Valentine's Day Massacre would take place fourteen years later. It is more common to hear the screams early in the morning, especially near the anniversary of the disaster.

Archer Woods Cemetery

Although this cemetery is not as well-known as the other more haunted graveyards in and around Chicago, Archer Woods Cemetery has had its share of ghosts and spirits. This is a fairly old cemetery that has somewhat fallen into disrepair over the last few decades. One ghost in particular is of a woman who only can be heard as you exit the cemetery. The woman's identity is not known, but the phenomenon has been told since at least the 1960s. People who pay their respects to friends and loved ones can sometimes hear a woman crying as they are about to leave the cemetery gates. There have also been reports of an old-fashioned horse-drawn hearse seen in front of the cemetery. This would make sense, since Archer Woods Cemetery has been in use since the early 1800s. In addition, people have seen floating lights or orbs dancing around late at night in the cemetery.

Bachelor's Grove Cemetery

Bachelor's Grove Cemetery has quite possibly one of the highest concentrations of hauntings of any location in the Chicago area. The cemetery was regularly used for over one hundred years, but after burials started to decrease in the 1960s, it became a regular place for teenagers to party.

In regard to paranormal activity, there appears to be no fewer than fourteen distinct entities at Bachelor's Grove Cemetery, although some estimate the number to be much higher. There are red and orange balls of light that are sometimes seen from within the cemetery that move rapidly from place to place. One possibility is that these are the ghostly impressions of the lanterns carried by the original groundskeepers at the cemetery. Most of the paranormal activity comes in the form of orbs, disembodied voices, or misty forms, but there are at least three specific ghosts that stand out from the rest.

A few years before the cemetery opened in 1844, a farmer owned the land adjacent to the cemetery. One day, he was plowing a garden when something spooked his horse. He lost control of the horse and it ran into a nearby pond. The man tried desperately to free the horse from the heavy plow equipment, but both the farmer and the horse drowned. The farmer and the horse can be seen at the edge of the cemetery.

The second spirit of Bachelor's Grove Cemetery is that of a woman who was buried next to her infant son. On clear moonlit nights, she can be seen walking through the cemetery as if she is looking for a particular gravesite. As she nears her tombstone, her apparition always disappears. Often, sounds of a baby crying and a woman singing softly to comfort the infant can be heard. Because she is always seen wearing a white dress, the ghost has been called the White Lady.

Perhaps the most peculiar apparitions in Bachelor's Grove Cemetery have been sightings of a small group of silent hooded figures. Most people who have seen them always say that there are three or four people dressed in monks' robes walking through the cemetery, apparently oblivious to their surroundings. It is possible that these hooded figures were from the monastery that was once used in the vicinity.

Although not part of Bachelor's Grove Cemetery, there is a nearby turnpike that has been the scene of several deadly car accidents over the years. There have been apparitions of cars accompanied by the sound of brakes screeching, only to disappear. Some of the people who died in these accidents may very well be buried behind the rusty gates of this graveyard.

Loyola University Chicago
1032 W. Sheridan Road

Loyola University was founded in 1870 under the name of St. Ignatius College. It wouldn't be known as Loyola University until thirty-nine years later in 1909. Today, it is largest Jesuit University in the United States. It has a long, proud history of producing successful graduates who have gone on to become great leaders, politicians, and lawyers. It has also produced its own share of ghost stories, including a pair of ghosts that haunt a building on the main campus.

In the early 1880s, when the college was still known as St. Ignatius College, a nun and Jesuit priest fell in love and had an affair. Shortly after they consummated their love, the nun discovered that she was pregnant and went to tell her lover. She told the priest that she loved him and that she would be willing to give up her position in the church if he would relinquish his title of priest. They could leave the college one night and start a new life in another city with their child. The priest refused her plan, saying that he could not turn his back on God. Grieving and heart-broken, the nun climbed thirteen floors of stairs in what is known today as the Skyscraper building and hung herself. After reconsidering her offer, the priest searched for the nun. Not knowing that she killed herself, the priest was horrified when he found her lifeless corpse swaying from the makeshift noose. When the priest realized what she had done, he was so overcome with grief that he opened a nearby window and jumped thirteen stories to his death. Their bodies were found the next morning.

The highest floors of the Skyscraper are now vacant, but students on campus can see a light flicker from the window to the room where the nun hanged herself. A few have claimed to have seen a form swaying from a noose in a window. Others report of hearing a man's sobbing, and a short scream followed by a sudden silence.

Mount Carmel Cemetery
1400 South Wolf Road

Located in the Chicago suburb of Hillside, Mount Carmel Cemetery is the final resting place of some of Chicago's most notorious gangsters, including Al Capone. The Catholic cemetery was consecrated in 1901 and is Chicago's largest, with more than 200,000 people buried there. Although Al Capone is buried in the cemetery, there have been no known reports of his ghost being seen in the graveyard. However, Mount Carmel Cemetery does have a spirit that has become known as the "Italian Bride."

Julia Buccola Petta was born in 1892 and died twenty-nine years later while giving birth to a child. Distraught, the family decided to erect a life-size statue of Petta wearing a wedding dress at her gravesite. At the base of the monument is a wedding photograph of Petta.

Within a few days of Petta's burial, her mother began to have disturbing dreams in which Julia was still alive. In the 1800s, people who had slipped into a coma were sometimes buried alive. As a precaution, a bell was sometimes placed beside the freshly dug grave with a string attached to inside the casket. If a person regained consciousness, he or she could ring the bell and the groundskeeper could commence to digging the person out of the grave. This is where the term "graveyard shift" originated. Whether Julia Petta had such a device attached to her gravestone is not known.

Julia Petta's mother continued to have these disturbing dreams for about six years. Eventually, Julia's mother was able to get permission to exhume her daughter's remains. To everybody's surprise, Julia's body showed no signs of decay. It was as if she had just been buried the day before. A photograph of the body was taken and placed on the front of the monument, replacing the wedding photo, where it remains to this day.

Not only was her body deemed incorruptible after six years, several stories surrounding Julia Petta and her ghost have emerged over the years. Several people, including many police officers patrolling the cemetery, have reported white mists or orbs near Petta's monument. Other people have claimed to have noticed the strong aroma of fresh-cut roses from near the monument throughout the year. An apparition fitting the description of Julia Petta wearing her bridal dress has also been seen wandering the cemetery close to her monument. Occasionally, the form will kneel in front of the monument as if she is placing flowers before fading away.

Wrigley Field
1060 West Addison Street

Wrigley Field was built in 1914 and has been the home of the Chicago Cubs since 1916. The ballpark was originally named Weeghman Park after Charles Weeghman, owner of the Chicago Whales. In 1915, William Wrigley Jr., of Wrigley's Spearmint Gum fame, obtained controlling interest in the newly formed Chicago Cubs and the park in 1918, and in 1926 renamed the park after himself.

One side-note is that in the 1980 movie *The Blues Brothers*, Dan Ackroyd (Elwood Blues) provides the address 1060 West Addison Street as his home address on his driver's license. Only when police attempt to find Elwood do they realize that he used the address for Wrigley Field. Way to go, Elwood!

Wrigley Field is reportedly one of the most haunted baseball parks in the world. Some believe that several of baseball's greats loved the game and the park so much that they decided to stay there long after they died.

Charlie Grimm was a player and manager of the Chicago Cubs in the 1930s and 1940s. Under his management, the Cubs won National League championships in 1932, 1935, and 1945. Although Grimm worked with other baseball teams over the years (notably the Pittsburgh Pirates, the Dallas Eagles, and the Milwaukee Brewers), his favorite team was the Chicago Cubs. There is no doubt that Charlie Grimm loved baseball. According to legend, Grimm loved Wrigley Field and the Chicago Cubs so much that he had his ashes secretly buried in left field of Wrigley Stadium when he died in 1983.

Since Grimm's death, security guards have heard the bullpen telephone ringing from the dugout in the middle of the night. When the guards go to investigate, the dugout is usually empty, although there have been reports of an apparition that looks remarkably like Charlie Grimm that can be seen walking the dugout and the hallways at night.

Another famous Chicago Cubs personality that haunts Wrigley Stadium is the one and only Harry Caray. Caray had an impressive career as a sportscaster that spanned nearly fifty years. Caray got his start in 1945 with the St. Louis Browns and worked for various baseball teams until he finally decided to be the voice for the Chicago Cubs. He worked for the team for sixteen seasons, and in the process made himself a permanent fixture at Wrigley Field and Chicago. Not long after his death in 1998, Caray's ghost started to be seen sitting in the press box and walking the bleachers of Wrigley Field.

Rosehill Cemetery
5800 North Ravenswood Ave.

The original name of this 450-acre cemetery was to be Roe's Hill, named after a local farmer who had land adjacent to the site. However, a typographical error renamed it Rosehill Cemetery. People liked the new name better and as a result, it has been known as Rosehill Cemetery ever since. The cemetery dates back to 1859 and several notable Chicago figures are buried there, including several former mayors of Chicago and governors of Illinois. Charles Hull, associated with the formation of Hull House mentioned earlier in this chapter, is also buried here.

In May 1864, twenty-year-old Frances Pearce died while giving birth to her daughter. It was likely not the childbirth that was fatal for Frances, but the fact that she may have been weakened by tuberculosis. The infant daughter was named Frances to honor her deceased mother. Unfortunately, the baby died about four months later and was buried beside her mother in Rosehill Cemetery. After they were buried together, there have been several reports of a woman heard either laughing or crying. Sometimes when the monument is photographed, an image of a woman holding an infant can sometimes appear in the picture.

Richard Sears, founder of Sears, Roebuck and Co. died in 1914 and was laid to rest inside a crypt at Rosehill Cemetery. After Sears's death, people began to see him walking near his crypt in the formal attire and top hat

The Chicago Water Tower
(image courtesy Library of Congress)

he was buried in. Another ghost that has been seen inside Rosehill Cemetery is that of the cemetery's original designer, William Boyington. This famous designer was also responsible for the design of the famous Chicago Water Tower, where a fireman's ghost can be seen hanging from a window. Boyington died in 1898, and one of his dying wishes was to be buried in a crypt that reflected the architectural style that was used for Rosehill Cemetery, the Chicago Water Tower, and several other Chicago buildings. Unfortunately, after the crypt was designed, it was unable to be finished based on Boyington's wishes, and his family had no choice but to design something much more ordinary. It undoubtedly would have upset Boyington had he known that his final wishes could not be fulfilled. This may be the reason why, to this day, people can still hear sounds of construction and a person moaning from within the walls of Boyington's crypt.

Clarendon Hills

Country House
241 West 55th Street

There are a two versions as to what happened that led to the Country House to become haunted. The first version of the story is that in the 1950s, a local resident had an affair with a bartender at the Country House. She had an illegitimate child with the bartender, who refused to claim the infant daughter as his own. One night, the woman and the bartender got into a heated argument and she left the restaurant with her daughter. In her rage, the mother put her daughter in her vehicle and sped out from the restaurant's parking lot. She lost control of the vehicle and hit a tree about a half mile from the restaurant. The mother died in the accident, but the daughter survived. The bartender felt responsible for the woman's death, took custody of the daughter and raised her as his own.

The second account is very similar, but has a few twists. In this version, a young mother entered the bar with her daughter late one night and asked the bartender to watch her while she ran some errands. In this version, there is no mention of an affair or that the bartender even knew the woman. The bartender refused because he felt that the mother was simply going to abandon the child and never return. The woman got mad and sped away in the car with her daughter. The car hit a tree about a mile from the restaurant, killing both the mother and her daughter. There is speculation that the mother had intentionally crashed her car into the tree, but since she died at the scene, nobody can be for certain.

No matter which version you choose to believe, one thing is certain … the ghosts of the woman and her daughter have been haunting the Clarendon Hills Country House for nearly fifty years. Although the haunting mostly consists of slamming doors, broken dishes and plates, lights turning on and off by themselves, and shutters opening suddenly, there have been sightings of a misty form of a woman holding her young daughter at both the bar and the entrance to the restaurant. On occasion, there have also been the sounds of a crying baby. If a person stands outside the restaurant and listens, the sounds of screeching brakes followed by a loud crash can sometimes be heard down the road.

Justice
················

Resurrection Cemetery

7201 Archer Avenue

According to legend, in 1934 a teenage girl was killed in a car accident on her way home from nearby Willowbrook Ballroom. Although her identity was thought to have been lost over the years, most people who have thoroughly studied the legend of Resurrection Mary believe that the ghost can be identified as a teenager named Mary Bregovy, who died in a horrible automobile accident in 1934.

The most common version of the origin of Resurrection Mary is that Mary and her boyfriend got into a fight on a cold winter's night and she walked home from the Willowbrook, or O'Henry, Ballroom. She was wearing a white, flowing ball gown. The gown blended in with the snow, so it was difficult for passing motorists to see her walking along the side of the road. Mary was hit by a speeding car and the driver left the scene, leaving her to die cold and alone in a roadside ditch. Her body was found the next morning. Mary's parents arranged to have her buried at Resurrection Cemetery, near where the accident occurred. They buried her in the white dress that she died in.

Shortly after her death in 1934, hundreds of drivers have seen Mary Bregovy's ghost walking along Archer Avenue leading to Resurrection Cemetery. Generally, the driver is traveling along Archer Avenue late at night when he or she sees a young woman wearing a white dress hitching a ride. The car pulls over and the girl gets into the front seat. Mary will give directions to where she needs to be dropped off, which is inevitably Resurrection Cemetery. At this point, she will either disappear right before the driver's eyes, or she will walk up to and through the cemetery gate.

Joliet

....

Rialto Square Theater

15 East Van Buren

The Rialto Square Theater opened in May 1926 and was originally to be opened as a vaudeville theater. Over the years, the venue not only was a movie theater, but also served as a a stage theater and a concert hall. There have been hundreds of world-famous acts that have performed at the Rialto, ranging from the comedy of the Marx Brothers and Ron White to the musical talents of Johnny Cash and Alice Cooper.

The architecture can be described as nothing short of breathtaking, with very ornate Duchess Chandeliers, marble walls in the lobby, and a magnificent domed ceiling. There is no wonder that the Rialto has become known as the "Jewel of Joliet" and is on the American Institute of Architects's list of the 150 great places in Illinois.

With such a history, it's understandable that people would want to stay at the Rialto after they have died. Employees, performers, and visitors have had very similar accounts of ghostly activity over the years. In addition to the typical voices, cold spots, and electrical problems that often accompany haunted areas, the Rialto has at least two paranormal acts that have yet to be canceled.

One haunting is of a couple that has been seen and photographed several times in the theater's balcony. Some people say that not long after the Rialto opened in 1926, a man and woman were in the balcony during a performance. They got too close to the edge and fell off the balcony to their deaths. Although these ghosts are silent, there is often a persistent cold spot in the balcony where they were sitting. There are no documented cases of a couple falling to their deaths in the history of the Rialto, however. It could be just as likely that the ghosts are of two theatergoers who particularly enjoy the view from the balcony.

Another ghost is that of a woman described to be in her mid-twenties that has been seen both backstage and near the theater's giant organ. When she is experienced or photographed, it is described as a misty or vaporous form. The working hypothesis of this ghost's origin is that it is of an actress that performed at the Rialto in the 1920s.

Frank Shaver Allen House
Corner of Morgan and Dewey

Frank Shaver Allen was a prominent architect known throughout Illinois for his work. Two of his structures, Kenosha High School and the English High Gothic Revival–style Christ Episcopal Church in Joliet, have been placed on the National Register of Historic Places. Although he was a well-known architect, the house that he lived in has become famous for quite another reason.

In 1934, F. S. Allen died at the age of seventy-four of natural causes while living in Pasadena, California. After his death, several private residents have lived in the nondescript, well-built house on the corner of Morgan and Dewey Streets. In the 1970s, the Frank Shaver Allen house became quite the media focal point when the residents invited a local newspaper reporter and some talented psychics into the house to investigate the ghosts that had been haunting it for years. The homeowners' claims to the paranormal activity that had taken place were nothing more than remarkable for the reporter, who started the investigation a skeptic and left a believer.

The psychics claimed to have encountered several ghosts when they investigated the house. One of the ghosts in the house is likely that of Frank Shaver Allen himself, who was often found to be in one of the front rooms of the home. The psychics also were able to communicate with an elderly woman who died in the house after a long illness, a young boy, and a housekeeper or nanny. Skeptical, the reporter researched the house and discovered that people who fit those descriptions had lived there over the years. According to the psychics, there were other spirits who were unable to be identified.

Visitors and residents of the house have claimed to have seen these spirits since the late 1930s. In addition to the ghosts in the front rooms, there have been sightings of fires burning in different places throughout the house. When a person went to investigate the fires, they would disappear. The smell of burning wood would sometimes be noticed long after the phantom fire had disappeared.

Joliet Arsenal/Joliet Army Ammunition Plant

Joliet Arsenal was constructed in two separate locations (the Kankakee Ordnance Works and the Elwood Ordnance Plant) in 1940. In 1945, the two locations were decommissioned and later combined to form the Joliet Army Ammunition Plant, which was used during World War II to produce TNT and other munitions necessary to help American soldiers win the war. After World War II ended, the production of munitions were halted. The Joliet Army Ammunition Plant resumed production of munitions for the Korean War and the Vietnam War, but it was permanently closed in the 1980s during the Reagan Administration.

On June 5, 1942, a large explosion at the Elwood Ordnance Plant killed forty-eight workers. The explosion was so destructive that it could be felt more than sixty miles away and the damage was so extensive that many of the workers' bodies were never recovered. The only reason that there was not more death and destruction was that the munitions plant was actually at two separate sites. If there had been only one central location, the explosion could have caused a chain reaction that would have been much more costly in terms of loss of life and physical damage.

Today, there is little left to show where the arsenal actually stood. Those who know how to get there often claim to hear noises of machinery running. They have also reported hearing the sound of vehicles speeding off although there are no cars nearby.

Bloomington
....

Illinois Wesleyan University—
Kemp Hall/International House

1312 N Park St

Illinois Wesleyan University was founded in 1850 and is associated with the United Methodist Church.

One building on the Bloomington campus has been the source of a ghost story that simply will not die. The International House was officially made part of the campus in 1912, and was named after Theodore Kemp, the eighth college president. While he was president of Illinois Wesleyan University, Kemp used the mansion as his private residence.

There are at least two ghosts associated with the International House. The first ghost is that of a young girl who has been seen wandering the halls on the third floor. Generally, her apparition will appear walking down the hallway and will disappear after a few seconds. She appears to be oblivious to the current students living in this dormitory. Occasionally, rather than seeing the ghost, residents can sometimes hear a girl laughing. Apparently, when the International House was a private residence, the school president's daughter would often be found playing on this floor. Most people tend to surmise that the ghost is actually that of the president's daughter, who allegedly died on the third floor of the mansion.

Shortly after the turn of the twentieth century, an elevator was installed in the International House. One day, a male resident decided to ride the elevator down from the top to the ground floor. Apparently, the elevator got stuck. Not long after, the cables holding the elevator snapped, causing it to crash into the basement. The young man died in the accident. For safety purposes, the elevator shaft was sealed off from the rest of the dormitory. However, every semester several students who reside at the International House claim to hear the snap of the cable, the grinding of the elevator as it plummets, and the crash in the basement. There have not been reported apparitions for this haunting.

Spontaneous Human Combustion

Not only are there ghosts in the Bloomington area, but there are also other reports of paranormal activity, including spontaneous human combustion. For those unfamiliar with the phenomenon, this means sometimes a person will literally catch fire for no apparent reason. The person is not close to a heat source and there is no accelerant, such as gasoline, nearby. The person literally bursts into flames. Sometimes, the person simply has a few severe burns and survives the experience. More likely, the person will succumb to the flames and literally be burned to ashes. Although not a common occurrence (there have only been a little over two hundred documented reports in the last three hundred years), spontaneous human combustion does in fact happen. At least one of the two hundred documented cases of human combustion took place in downtown Bloomington, Illinois.

In 1942, Aura Troyer was a janitor at a bank in downtown Bloomington. He was in the basement doing his job when some coworkers suddenly heard him start to scream in pain. When they ran down to the basement, Troyer was already consumed by fire, and most of his clothing had already been burnt. The man screamed that it happened all of a sudden. Before the fire could be extinguished by his coworkers, Troyer died from the flames. There was no record of Troyer being a smoker, and there were no combustible chemicals near him. It should also be noted that although Troyer died in the fire, nothing else nearby ever caught fire.

Springfield

Springfield Theatre Centre
420 S. Sixth Street

The Springfield Theatre Centre was established in 1947 as a community theater that held plays and other performances for the citizens of Springfield, Illinois. The shows held at the Springfield Theatre Centre have entertained thousands of people in the nearly seventy years since it opened its doors. Some believe that it just also happens to be haunted by an actor who committed suicide.

Joe Neville became a regular performer at the Springfield Theatre Centre shortly after it opened. Although he had a generally dour disposition and few people really enjoyed his company, there was little argument that he was a very good actor. Neville's colleagues overlooked his arrogance and snide remarks because they knew they could rely on him to give a memorable performance on stage.

Joe would often brag about how he had been professionally trained and had traveled Europe in the years immediately following World War II. Although this may have been the case, he was never able to provide any documentation to support his claims or even that he had been to Europe at all.

In addition to a love for theater, he also had a love for money. Eventually, Joe began to embezzle large sums of money from his place of employment. After doing an audit, Joe's boss discovered this and called the police. After a brief investigation, there was enough evidence to arrest Joe for embezzlement.

Joe caught wind of his impending arrest the evening prior to the opening night of *Mr. Barry's Etchings*. Essentially, the play is a comedy about a gifted artist who inadvertently becomes a counterfeiter by making an etching of a fifty dollar bill so perfect that it could fool the experts. Appropriately, Joe Neville had been given the lead role. Although most accounts indicate that the play was performed in 1951, the official Springfield Theatre Centre website indicated that *Mr. Barry's Etchings* was actually performed during the 1954–1955 season.

Joe never let on to the other actors that he was about to be arrested for embezzlement. After the final dress rehearsal, Joe went quietly to his home and took a bottle of painkillers. When the police found him the next day, Joe had been dead for several hours. When the other actors had learned of his fate, they did not mourn; rather, they found an understudy to replace Joe's role and continued the show the following night.

When Joe died, and his will was read before the beneficiaries, he had bequeathed several extraordinary items such as land or castles to them. Their excitement soon turned to frustration when the beneficiaries attempted to claim ownership of the items that Joe had willed to them. Soon it was discovered that Neville never owned any property or other extravagant items promised in the will.

Immediately after Joe Neville's death, actors and other stagehands began to notice things were a bit out of the ordinary at the Springfield Theatre Centre. Large shadows were seen cast against the wall as if a person was standing in front of the floodlights. At other times, a shadowlike figure could be seen walking onstage, as if rehearsing blocking for a scene. It is believed that this is the ghost of Joe Neville because it was commonly known that he would often rehearse his roles long into the night after all of his colleagues went home.

Some employees claim that if you talk about Joe, he will likely attempt to make his presence known. Generally, this will be in the form of batteries being drained in electronic devices or overhead and stage lights turning on and off by themselves. In fact, there have been so many sightings of Joe over the years that he has finally become accepted by the actors who still put on plays and performances at the Springfield Theatre Centre. Perhaps in death, Joe finally found something that he could not find while alive ... acceptance.

Dana-Thomas House
301 East Lawrence Avenue

The Dana Thomas house was designed and built by world-renowned architect Frank Lloyd Wright in 1902. Wright was known for attempting to blend his buildings into the landscape. Perhaps one of the best examples of this architectural style is Falling Water in Mill Run, Pennsylvania.

One of the first people to live in the house at 301 East Lawrence Avenue was Susan Lawrence Dana, a young and well-to-do Springfield socialite who was known to throw expensive and lavish parties as well as make considerable donations to various charities in the Springfield area.

Over the years, Susan Dana had her share of sadness and death. Her first husband died in 1900 while inspecting a mine. Her second husband died unexpectedly in 1913. In addition, she had two children who did not survive infancy. Although both husbands died suddenly, there was no reason to believe that foul play ever played a part in either death.

Likely as a result of these losses, Susan Dana became extremely interested in the Spiritualism movement of the 1920s. She invited several psychics and mediums from all over Illinois and nearby states for elaborate parties and séances in an attempt to communicate with the dead, particularly her dead husbands, father, and children. She became so consumed with the paranormal and metaphysical that she formed the Lawrence Center for Constructive Thoughts in the late 1920s. Susan Dana was still well-known for hosting lavish parties, but rather than hosting them for the community's political elite, she hosted them for people that she thought could help her communicate with spirits from the afterlife.

Finally, after a cousin that was living with her died, Susan Dana moved into another, more modest house. Although she loved the house she had lived in for so many years on East Lawrence Avenue, she had spent most of her money and simply had to find a less expensive place to live. Susan Dana lived in the house until 1928, but sold it to Charles Thomas shortly before she was declared incompetent and sent to a local nursing hospital, where she died in 1946.

Shortly after her death, the new residents began to hear a variety of voices from different parts of the house, particularly in the parlors where the séances were known to have been held. On tours of the home today, people notice cold spots throughout the house. Others have noticed out of their peripheral vision people sitting in some of the original furnishings from the house. When they turn around to look at the people, the chair or couch is empty. There is no indication that the house is haunted by Susan Dana. There have been no direct apparitions of Susan Dana or anybody else reported. Although it could be Susan's ghost at the house, it could just as likely be haunted by many of her guests to the parties or séances that were held at the house over the years.

The Inn at 835
835 South Second Street

The Inn at 835 is one of six luxury apartment buildings that were arranged to be built by Bell Miller. She became very successful as a florist, eventually amassing a great deal of wealth. This particular apartment building was constructed in 1909. In the 1990s, the apartments were converted into guest rooms, and the place now functions as a bed-and-breakfast.

There is reason to believe that of the six apartment buildings, the Inn at 835 was perhaps Bell Miller's favorite. Guests in one of the seven bedrooms have seen a person walking past their doorway, have noticed the overwhelming scent of fresh-cut flowers, and have heard a pleasant voice in conversation or song. In addition, in one of the sitting rooms, there is a bookcase that has books of all kinds placed tightly together on its shelves. However, when a person will sometimes leave the sitting room for a short time or even turns in another direction, upon return a book is always found on the table. There is no way that the book could have fallen.

Carlinville

Loomis House
112 North Side Square

The Loomis House was built by Judge Thaddeus Loomis in 1870. It was originally opened as a fifty-room hotel, which was being built at the same time as the town's new courthouse. Although Loomis had been considered by most to be an honest man, public opinion began to sway in the other direction when the estimated cost of the new courthouse kept on increasing. Citizens began to speculate that the money being allocated to the courthouse building fund was actually going to build Loomis's hotel. There was plenty of reason to believe that this was actually the case. The same limestone that was being used for the courthouse was also being used for the hotel. The man who designed the courthouse was also hired to design the hotel. In addition, the final cost of the courthouse was an amazing $1,342,000, which would be the equivalent of over $39 million today! Loomis was accused of corruption and embezzlement. The only thing that he did admit to was that he had used the limestone left over from the courthouse for the construction of his hotel. Although he did say that he obtained the limestone legally, Loomis was never able to provide documentation to substantiate his claims. After a drawn-out legal proceeding, Judge Loomis had been cleared of any formal charges simply due to lack of evidence. However, he was never looked at the same way by the citizens of Carlinville.

After the legal battles ended, Judge Loomis decided to focus on making his hotel a success. In 1881, it was determined that the bar owner who had an establishment inside the hotel had violated Illinois liquor laws and was forced to close. Without the income from the bar, business dwindled down to nearly nothing—to the point that less than ten years after the hotel's construction Loomis was forced to close the hotel and sell the building. When the hotel was reopened six months later, it was renamed the St. George Hotel in an effort to remove any association with the former judge from it.

Although there were several businesses in the building over the years, in the 1950s the upper floors of the hotel were in such disrepair that several rooms on the upper two floors were unusable. In 1975, the hotel changed hands again and the new owner renamed the hotel the Loomis House. The top two floors were renovated, the bottom floor had been opened as a bar, and the second floor had been converted into an upscale restaurant, which has since closed. Only after the extensive conversion of the second floor into the restaurant did the ghosts of the Loomis House make themselves known.

There are at least two ghosts haunting the Loomis House. First, there have been sightings of an older man standing in the dining room before the restaurant opened for evening hours. When an employee would approach him to ask if he needed anything, the apparition would suddenly disappear. A second ghost is believed to be none other than Judge Loomis himself. Patrons of the downstairs bar have claimed to see a man dressed in nineteenth-century business attire with a long, thick beard. A photograph of Judge Loomis found in the courthouse matches the apparition seen in this part of the building.

MISSOURI

317 miles

Crossing from Illinois, Route 66 passes through 317 miles of Missouri. This state has quite a history in and of itself without taking into account the contributions of Route 66. Missouri also has its share of the paranormal, especially in many towns along the Mother Road. Some of these stories go back to a time before there even was a Route 66, a state of Missouri, or even a United States.

There are sections of Missouri that Route 66 once passed through that many of the indigenous Native American tribes thought of as being closer to the spirit world than others. With locations with names such as Zombie Road and several places that have had documented cases of intense paranormal activity, perhaps they were on to something.

41

St. Louis

....

Zombie Road

Lawler Ford Road

Long before American settlers arrived, the area now known as Zombie Road was visited by several Native American tribes, including the Osage, Adena, Miami, Shawnee, and Quapaw. The area was rich with wild game, fresh water was plentiful from the Meramec River, and a nearby natural flint quarry supplied them with material for arrows and spears.

The official name of Zombie Road is Lawler Ford Road. This narrow, two-mile stretch of road was originally built in the 1860s as an access road from the Meramec River to the nearby railroad. Both the road and railroad were primarily used to transport stone from the quarries to boats, which would then take it to cities all along the Meramec River.

With a name like Zombie Road, one would undoubtedly expect some paranormal activity—and it does!

There have been reports of strange happenings in the area since this area was settled. Although rich in many things that the tribes wanted, there was still something dark and foreboding about this area. For generations, there have been legends of bluish or yellow-white glowing lights being spotted on Zombie Road and throughout this region. The "spook lights," as they are called, have been described as large and silent, ranging in size from about that of a baseball to as large as two or three feet in diameter.

Many of the tribes that traveled through this part of Missouri have legends that explain the lights. One of the more common Native American legends is that the spook lights represent the spirit of an Osage or Quapaw warrior that was beheaded and is doomed to spend eternity looking for his own severed head.

The first documented report of this phenomenon was from a small book published in 1881 called *The Ozark Spook Lights*. However, most Native American tribes did not document events with specific dates;

rather their traditions and legends were generally passed down orally. Because of this, documenting the actually date of the first spook lights is virtually impossible.

A local tanner and leather worker by the name of Henry McCullough purchased some property along Zombie Road and made a very lucrative living by selling supplies to local quarry workers and shipping his wares downriver. In 1876, Henry McCullough's wife, Della, was killed after being hit by a railroad car. The accident was described as very gruesome and she reportedly had died instantly from the impact. Not long after Della's death, people began to hear a woman scream near the exact spot where the accident took place.

Lawler Ford Road was given the nickname of Zombie Road in the 1950s by local teenagers who partied there on weekends. After the early 1940s, people had primarily abandoned the area, including the summer beach houses. Although some of the beach houses were converted into permanent residences, most of the houses were simply left to the elements. Lawler Ford Road provided the perfect combination of Native American legends, sightings of unidentified lights, abandoned houses, and railroad tracks for fertile teenage imaginations to come up with the new, more sinister name of Zombie Road.

One ghost story that comes from Zombie Road is that of a woman who lived in one of the beach houses in the early 1930s. Not wanting trespassers, the woman was known for yelling at people who she felt came come too close to her property. Eventually, she died alone in her beach house—well after many people moved out, abandoned, or tore down their houses. There are those who say that if you travel down Zombie Road and approach the few abandoned beach houses that are partially standing, you can sometimes hear a woman's voice from one of the houses yelling at you.

Another Zombie Road ghost story is that of a man who was struck and killed by a train in the late 1960s while walking on the railroad track late one night. His ghost is sometimes seen walking along what is left of the old railroad tracks. He is described as relatively young, wearing a sweater, looking down with his hands in his pockets. To this day, the man's identity remains a mystery.

While doing research on Zombie Road, I couldn't help but notice the similarities between this road and the TNT area just outside of Point Pleasant, West Virginia. During World War II, the area was used to create and stockpile explosives for the war effort. After the war ended, the place was largely abandoned and the buildings where the explosives were stored, known as igloos, were left to the elements. In the 1950s and 1960s, teenagers would go to the TNT area to party. One night in the summer of 1967, four teenagers were driving when they saw a large creature with large, batlike wings and glowing red eyes. They outran the creature, which followed them out of the TNT area. Over the next several weeks, there were over 100 other sightings of the creature that became known as Mothman, which ended after the Silver Bridge collapsed on December 15, 1967. For a more detailed account, check out Jeff Wamsley's book *Mothman: The Facts Behind the Legend*, or John Keel's *The Mothman Prophecies*.

Lemp Mansion
3322 DeMenil Place

Lemp Mansion was a 9,015-square-foot mansion built in 1868 by Jacob Feickert and was purchased eight years later by wealthy businessman William J. Lemp, whose father, John Adam Lemp, made a fortune first as a grocery store owner and then as the founder of Lemp Brewery. According to the official Lemp Mansion website, Lemp Brewery spanned five city blocks and was worth an estimated $7 million dollars in the late 1800s.

After William Lemp purchased the mansion, he made major renovations to several rooms to accommodate offices for the brewery. Although it is one of the most beautiful buildings in the St. Louis area, Lemp Mansion carries with it a very macabre and tragic history that involves at least seven deaths.

The first death associated with Lemp Mansion was William Lemp's son, Frederick. On December 21, 1901, just four days before Christmas, Frederick was found dead inside the mansion by his father. Although Frederick did have considerable health problems from childhood that continued into adulthood, he died at the relatively young age of twenty-eight. Because Frederick was so young, some speculated that he may have been murdered. However, there was nothing to indicate that a crime had been committed. All the same, an official cause of death was never released and he was quietly buried in the family mausoleum in the nearby Calvary Cemetery. As we will find out later, this is not the only secret this family's mausoleum holds.

Only three years after Frederick's death, William J. Lemp Sr. took a Smith and Wesson .38 revolver and shot himself in the side of the head. He was pronounced dead at exactly 10:15 a.m., February 13, 1904. There was no suicide note or any explanation as to why he would choose to kill himself, although most speculate that he never really recovered from the suicide of his youngest son, Frederick.

The family history became more tragic in 1920 when William Lemp's daughter, Elsa, also committed suicide. As with the other suicide, there does not appear to be a record of Elsa leaving a suicide note. It was commonly known that Elsa and her husband had a troubled marriage. In February 1919, Elsa filed for divorce. The divorce was granted, but Elsa reconciled with her husband in March 1920. Less than a month after deciding to get back with her husband, Elsa was dead by her own hand. Although there was a reconciliation and a renewal of vows, Elsa's relationship with her husband was still very turbulent.

After moving back in with her husband in March 1920, Elsa started to show signs of severe depression and insomnia. She would often be seen walking through her house at all hours while her husband slept in their bed. Elsa was up late one night thinking about her husband and their future together when she decided to take care of her relationship problems and her insomnia once and for all. During the pre-dawn hours of March 20, 1920, Elsa lay down in bed beside her husband and shot herself in the heart. The loud gunshot awakened her husband, but she had bled to death before he could do anything to save her.

Prohibition was partially to blame for the family downfall and yet another Lemp death in the early 1920s. Enacted in 1919, Prohibition eventually led to the ultimate downfall of the Lemp Brewery dynasty. The man in charge of Lemp Brewery at this time was William's son, William "Billy" Lemp Jr. Rather than reinvest the money into other ventures, Billy simply allowed the company to deteriorate and eventually sold it for a fraction of what it had been worth. According to records, prior to Prohibition, Lemp Brewery was worth an estimated $7 million dollars. However, Billy Lemp sold the entire company for approximately $588,000 to the International Shoe Company. Less than two years after his sister Elsa killed herself, Billy Lemp killed himself on December 29, 1922. Ironically, Billy's suicide was almost identical in every way to his father's suicide twenty-one years before. Both had killed themselves in the same room, both used a pistol, and in both cases, neither had left a suicide note.

Perhaps one of the most interesting people to have ever lived at the Lemp Mansion was William Lemp Jr's ex-wife, Lillian. Born in 1877, Lillian married William Jacob Lemp Jr. in 1899 at the age of twenty-two. It was no secret that her favorite color was lavender; she was known to dress only in the color lavender for every occasion. Locals began to refer to Lillian Lemp as The Lavender Lady. The only time that Mrs. Lemp did not wear lavender was when she was going through the divorce proceedings with William J. Lemp in 1908.

In addition to being blamed for selling Lemp Brewery for a fraction of its actual worth, it appears that Billy Lemp had quite an active social life that resulted in the birth of at least one illegitimate child. It has been rumored that Billy was having a relationship of convenience with one of the servants. Soon after the affair began, the servant discovered that she was pregnant. The child allegedly was born with Down syndrome or a similar genetic condition and did not live more than ten years. Although this rumor has never been substantiated, there reportedly is an unmarked child's grave at the Lemp Mausoleum in the Calvary Cemetery about nine miles from the mansion.

It seemed that with Billy Lemp's death, the so-called Lemp curse had claimed its last victim. Sadly, that was not to be the case. William Sr.'s third son, Charles, moved into the mansion shortly after his brother Billy's suicide. He became more angry and isolated over the family's financial problems until, on May 10, 1949, he followed suit with other family members and committed suicide in the mansion. Of the four Lemp suicides, Charles was the only one to leave a suicide note. A man of few words, Charles's note simply read, *"In case I am found dead, blame it on no one but me. Ch. A. Lemp."*

After Charles Lemp died in 1949, the mansion was auctioned off and eventually became a boarding house in 1950. The boarding house only had mediocre success, partly because of the deaths associated with it as well as whispers from many of the boarders that there was something ghostly going on within its walls. The Lemp Mansion had gained the reputation of being haunted, and this attracted the attention of psychics from across the country. The owners had arranged to have these psychics conduct a series of séances in different rooms in the mansion. Although several of the psychics did not know each other and were given very little information about the mansion before the séance, their intuitions independently led each to the rooms where at least three of the Lemps had dispatched themselves over the previous fifty years.

Several rooms in Lemp Mansion are reported to be haunted by the ghosts of several members of the Lemp family. According to the official website for Lemp Mansion, four rooms are hotspots for paranormal activity. Although Mrs. Lemp lived a full life and died of natural causes in 1960, she made such an impression at the Lemp Mansion that she reportedly haunts one of the rooms at the mansion today. To pay homage to Mrs. Lemp's favorite color, the room that Mrs. Lemp stayed in when she lived at Lemp Mansion is referred to today as The Lavender Suite. The William Lemp suite was originally an office for the Lemp Brewery Company and was also the room where William Lemp fatally shot himself. The Charles Lemp Suite is named after the third member of the Lemp family who committed suicide. The Elsa Lemp Suite is another room that guests report is haunted. Although Elsa Lemp did commit suicide, she did not do so at the mansion. Nevertheless, this room, located on the top floor of the mansion, was reported to be Elsa Lemp's bedroom when she lived at the mansion. Finally, the Louis and Frederick Lemp Suites are two adjoining rooms that were the former servants' quarters.

Most of the rooms that a person can stay in overnight have had paranormal activities associated with them. Window curtains and doors have been known to open and close when nobody is in the room. Unexplained loud crashes in the middle of the night will cause guests to wake up from a deep sleep. Perhaps most dramatic, in the rooms where William, Billy, Charles, and Frederick Lemp died, a loud gunshot can sometimes be heard.

There have been several reports of a child's presence felt in two parts of the mansion. Mostly, a little boy's face can be seen looking out an attic window. A young boy between six and ten years old has been seen in some of the rooms and the hallway on the second floor, where he was known to have played before he died.

As mentioned earlier, the Louis and Frederick Lemp suites were actually the old servants' quarters of the mansion. Some people who have stayed in these suites claim that they have had the uneasy feeling of being watched while they slept. Many believe that the ghost of the servant who gave birth to Billy Lemp's illegitimate child is here, constantly looking for her son, who is generally seen in the attic or the hallways.

Perhaps the most active of the spirits is that of Charles Lemp. Whereas the other ghosts found are generally confined to one or two areas, the ghost of Charles Lemp has been seen throughout the mansion. According to the trivia website, Charles Lemp is described as a short, thin man with straight, black hair wearing business attire from the early twentieth century. He has been seen in the room where he was found dead, in the hallways on at least two of the floors, and in the common living room of the mansion.

Today, Lemp Mansion is a bed-and-breakfast that hosts private parties, weddings, ghost hunts, murder-mystery weekends, and other activities for people from all walks of life.

Bissell Mansion
4426 Randall Place

The Bissel Mansion (image courtesy Barbara Schepker)

Bissell Mansion is one of the most well-known historical landmarks in the Saint Louis area not only because it is the city's oldest brick house still in use or the site of a successful dinner theater. It is also because it is believed that the mansion's namesake still resides there nearly one hundred and fifty years after his death.

Lewis Bissell came from a long line of military leaders, including his father, Major Russell Bissell, who was the first commander of Fort Bellafonte in St. Louis, Missouri. Lewis Bissell started his military career in 1808 when he was only nineteen years old and was promoted to the rank of Captain in 1815 at age twenty-six. After achieving the rank of Captain, Bissell was asked by the federal government to explore the wilderness of western Missouri and beyond in much the same way that Lewis and Clark had done several years previous.

Bissell explored the frontier for a few years, and upon returning to the St. Louis area started to purchase several tracts of land. A section of the property that he acquired along the Mississippi River is now known as Bissell Point. On one of these large tracts of land overlooking St. Louis, Bissell built a large brick mansion in 1823.

Captain Bissell died on November 25, 1868, at the age of seventy-nine in the mansion with some family members by his side and was buried in nearby Bellafonte Cemetery. For several years, there was little else to add to the story of Captain Lewis Bissell. However, that abruptly changed in 1958, when Bissell Mansion and other nearby historical buildings were in danger of being demolished as part of an urban renewal and beautification project for St. Louis. The plan was to level these historic buildings in order to remove the eyesores that many had become, or to simply build a new highway. After several local residents intervened by forming the Landmarks Association, Bissell Mansion and several other historic landmarks in St. Louis were saved and placed on the National Register of Historic Places.

In the 1980s, Bissell Mansion was purchased and eventually renovated into a restaurant. During the renovation, people began to notice small things such as equipment turning off or tools inexplicably coming up missing only to return a few hours or days later. Despite the delays caused by these problems, the mansion's renovations were completed. Today, Bissell Mansion is the site of a very popular restaurant and mystery dinner theater that has been featured in several entertainment and restaurant television shows and periodicals, including the Travel Channel and *Food and Wine* magazine.

After the restaurant opened, guests started to speak with management and staff about things they had seen. People have reported seeing the ghost of an older, distinguished-looking gentleman wearing a military uniform that some believe to be Lewis Bissell. He is always seen standing in the parking lot looking up toward his mansion. Although it is a parking lot today, when Bissell was alive, it is likely the spot where he had one of his many orchards that surrounded the house in the 1800s.

The ghost of woman has also been seen in one of the dining rooms and on the staircase leading to the second floor. She is consistently described as a young woman in her late twenties or early thirties wearing a long dress. Some people have mistaken her for an actress involved with the murder-mystery dinners or a comedy show. However, when she is approached, she always disappears. It is likely the ghost of one of Captain Bissell's wives, although her identity has not been confirmed. It should also be noted that none of the eyewitnesses have claimed to have felt any malevolence coming from Bissell's ghost. If anything, most people who encounter Captain Bissell get the impression that he is protective of his property and is keeping a vigilant eye on the mansion from beyond the grave.

Bridgeton

Payne-Gentry House
4211 Fee Fee Road

The Payne Gentry House was built in 1879 as the home of Elbridge Payne. Originally designed as a summer house by Payne and his family, he eventually moved in full time to raise his family in Bridgeton, Missouri. One of his children, William Payne, showed an interest in medicine from an early age and went to medical school when he grew up. Upon returning to Bridgeton after completing medical school, William Payne was given the house and opened a doctor's office in the basement. Although the original plan was for William to stay in the house only for a short time, Dr. Payne saw patients from all walks of life in his office for seventeen years.

During the late nineteenth century, there was a fairly high mortality rate with patients. During the seventeen years that he practiced medicine in the Payne-Gentry House, Dr. Payne undoubtedly had several patients die while under his care. This could be why some believe that the Payne-Gentry House is one of the most haunted places in Missouri.

According to the website *Haunted Missouri*, the Payne-Gentry House has as many as twenty separate entities. Chances are that they are the ghosts of patients that Dr. Payne treated while practicing medicine at the house. It is also likely that one of the ghosts that haunt the Payne-Gentry house is of the good doctor himself. Of all the ghosts reported at the Payne-Gentry House, the ghosts of a woman, a baby, and a dog are seen much more often than any of the others.

Over the years, there have been several sightings of a young woman who died in childbirth at the house. A baby's cry can be heard at all hours of the night and can be accompanied by a woman seen walking through the house. More often, the woman can be seen carrying a small bundle in her arms. Perhaps it is the ghost of the woman who died in childbirth and has finally reunited with her baby.

One of the most famous ghosts of the Payne-Gentry House is that of a dog. People who have taken the tours have stated that they have been followed by a dog who usually makes himself known by brushing up against unsuspecting members of the tour group. The person may look down to see the dog that nudged them only to find that there is nothing beside them. Others have claimed to see a dog lying down near a tree in the front yard of the house. When they go to check on the dog later, the dog has disappeared.

St. Charles

....

Across the Missouri River from St. Louis is the historic town of St. Charles, Missouri. It was founded in 1769 when a French-Canadian trapper named Louis Blanchette settled in the area. It is known as the starting point for several western explorers of the early 1800s, including Daniel Boone and Lewis and Clark. Once people started to settle out West, St. Charles became known as the starting point for the Santa Fe and Oregon Trails, both of which helped to settle the western part of the United States.

Lindenwood University
209 S Kingshighway Street

Lindenwood University was originally named the Linden Wood School for Girls when it was founded in 1827 by George and Mary Sibley. It is one of the oldest colleges located west of the Mississippi River.

Apparently, Mary Sibley was so dedicated to Lindenwood University that even death could not stop her from staying on campus. Although Mary Sibley died in 1878, she has been heard playing the pipe organ at the old Sibley Hall Chapel at all hours of the night. Old gospel hymns were Mary's choice of music and according to an article in the October 31, 2010, edition of the *Saint Louis Post-Dispatch*, Mary's ghost has a particular affinity to "Nearer My God to Thee." Of course, when night security or other curious bystanders try to discover who is playing the music, they are usually surprised to find the room that contains the organ locked up with the lights turned off.

Sibley Hall is not the only haunted area on campus. According to historical records, the present site of Cobbs Hall is where Mary Sibley had her garden when she was living on campus. Residents have claimed to have seen a woman wearing a white dress walking at the end of one of the halls. She is not seen very often at this location, but when she does make an appearance, her apparition is often accompanied by the smell of fresh-cut flowers.

South Main Street

400–700 South Main Street

With most hauntings, the apparitions or other ghostly activities tend to be isolated into a relatively small area, such as a hallway, a bedroom, or battlefield. However, there are exceptions. The 400–700 block area on South Main Street in St. Charles is one of those exceptions.

Today, South Main Street is a central location for tourists and local residents to visit. It hosts a variety of specialty shops, restaurants, lodging opportunities, taverns, and museums. Getting a feel for the culture and history that has made St. Charles famous requires spending an afternoon dining and shopping on South Main Street. However, there is a side of South Main Street that the average tourist may be unaware of. There are reports of dozens of different hauntings that occur in the businesses on South Main Street.

In 1853, it was decided that the Borromeo Cemetery be moved from its location on South Main Street to Randolph Street, nearly two miles inland because the cemetery's original site was too close to the Missouri River. Another hypothesis was that the property near the Missouri River was better suited for businesses than it was for a cemetery. The bodies were exhumed and moved farther back inland to Randolph Street. However, in the haste to move the bodies, some were lost in the transition, never to be found again.

Soon after people began to build on the site of the old cemetery, the ghostly activity began. Although there are only one or two buildings on the site of the old cemetery, a combination of moving long-dead bodies and construction may have been enough to stir up restless spirits that are still encountered to this day.

Today, the entire stretch of South Main Street is filled with dozens of curio shops that cater to the various tastes of visitors and tourists from all walks of life. There is a four-block section of South Main Street that also has a higher concentration of hauntings than perhaps all other parts of St. Charles, Missouri, combined.

The 400 block has several shops that at first glance would not seem to have any connection with the paranormal. However, there have been shop owners, staff, and customers who have heard strange scraping sounds coming from beneath the floors. Sometimes these sounds can be accompanied by the whispers of a few words spoken in either French or in a heavy French accent. Several businesses have also had reports of lights turning on and off as well as doors and windows opening and closing by themselves.

The 500 block of South Main Street appears to have the highest concentration of hauntings. A restaurant at 501 South Main Street is haunted by the ghosts of a man and woman from the mid-eighteenth century. Patrons and employees have seen apparitions on several different occasions over the years. They all describe the woman as very young and attractive, with shoulder-length hair and wearing a long dress. The man appears to be a bit older and has a more rugged appearance. Both appear to be wearing clothing that dates back to the late 1700s or early 1800s. Although they are most often seen separately, there have been some reports of the two apparitions being seen standing side by side.

According to many accounts, in the 1940s there was a kitchen fire at or near 519 South Main Street that killed a young girl who was trapped in the blaze. People at this location have claimed to have seen a girl about eight- to ten-years old wandering about on the first floor. Occasionally, the sound of a young girl can be heard speaking, but the voice is so quiet and soft that it is very difficult to make out what she is trying to say.

A third ghost that haunts a business on the 500 block of South Main Street belongs to an old riverboat captain. Long before this section of St. Charles became a tourist area, an old riverboat captain had a private residence at 523 South Main Street. When he was not piloting a riverboat, the captain liked to spend most of his time in a rocking chair on his porch. Today, the creaking sound of a rocking chair can be heard on the porch when nobody is around.

The 700 block of South Main Street is another hotspot for hauntings. Visitors who come to this area during the early morning hours will sometimes be greeted with the wonderful aroma of bread baking or a simmering stew, even though none of the businesses had started cooking. In addition to the aromas, the disembodied voices of people in conversation can be heard in this area. As with the 400-block haunting, the voices heard in this section appear to be speaking in French or with a heavy French accent.

Goldenrod Showboat
St. Charles, Missouri/Kampsville, Illinois

The Goldenrod Showboat has had quite an adventure since it was constructed in 1909. It was built in a time when the glamour of the showboat's mobile entertainment was starting to wane. Although times and people's taste in entertainment were changing, the 200-foot Goldenrod was one of the final showboats ever to be constructed at a cost of nearly $75,000—equivalent to about $1.6 million today.

Although this was a hefty sum, the Goldenrod Showboat was still successful. During its ten years of performing high-quality shows for audiences of all kinds, it was known to have a wide variety of vaudeville, musical, and other forms of entertainment. Famous acts such as Bob Hope and Red Skelton were known to perform onstage on several occasions while the Goldenrod was still providing shows on the Missouri and Mississippi Rivers. It has been estimated that the showboat could hold as many as 1,400 guests at one time, and on most nights, the shows were performed in front of sold-out audiences.

The Goldenrod's success was fairly short-lived and it was docked by the early 1920s. Soon after, the Goldenrod was nearly forgotten. A fire in 1962 almost destroyed the entire boat, but it was able to be salvaged.

The Goldenrod was purchased and renovated in 1989 and placed on the shores of the Missouri River in St. Charles, Missouri, where it again provided entertainment for people from all across the United States.

From 1990 to 2002, the Goldenrod drew crowds from across the country for several years until it was donated to the Lewis and Clark Landing in 2002.

Unfortunately, if somebody drove to St. Charles today to find the showboat, they would be very disappointed. After it was donated in 2002, it was eventually relocated nearly seventy-five miles to the north in Kampsville, Illinois, where it is currently docked on the Illinois River. Although this is the case, I decided to include the showboat in St. Charles because the town has become such an integral part of the showboat's history.

The ghost associated with the Goldenrod Showboat is a young, attractive woman who is always seen wearing a red dress. According to most accounts, when the Goldenrod was still traveling on the rivers as a showboat, one of the workers and his daughter lived on the boat. Being around the shows performed on the Goldenrod day after day, the daughter became enamored by what she saw and decided to become a performer on a showboat one day, although her father warned her that the days of the showboat industry were numbered.

While docked in St. Louis one night, the daughter once again approached her father about her desire to enter show business. He again disagreed with that career decision, and the two began to argue loudly. She left the showboat in a rage. Her father did not follow her, thinking that she just needed some time to calm down and come to her senses. However, it was the last time that he would see his daughter, Rose, alive.

The next morning, the father was approached by the captain of the Goldenrod. He told the father that his daughter had been brutally attacked by unknown assailants and was found floating face down in the river. Until the day he died, less than a year later, the father never got over the untimely death of his daughter.

Shortly after the father's death, guests, staff, and performers started to notice hints of Rose's presence on the Goldenrod. Usually, she makes herself known by closing doors and moving items. However, Rose's apparition has been seen several times over the years. She is often seen shortly before a show and is always seen wearing the same long dress that she was wearing the night she died. People who encountered her long after Rose and her father died were unaware of the story associated with her death. As the story continued to be told and more people had their own experience with the ghosts of the Goldenrod, the name Rose was all but forgotten. Because staff on the Goldenrod did not know Rose's true identity, her ghost was given the nickname of "Victoria."

Sullivan

Meramec Caverns
I-44 Exit 230

Route 66 was famous for having several one-of-a-kind tourist attractions. None may be as unique as the 4.6-mile underground cavern system known as Meramec Caverns located just outside of Sullivan, Missouri. If not the most unique attraction, it certainly is the oldest. Meramec Caverns has been estimated to be up to four million years old.

During the heyday of Route 66, Meramec Caverns had dozens of billboards erected in several states surrounding Missouri. This made Meramec Caverns a must-see while traveling the Mother Road. In addition, to promote the caverns, owner Lester Dill invented the bumper sticker. Today, Meramec Caverns draws as many as 150,000 visitors per year.

Hundreds of years ago, nomadic Native American tribes used the caverns for shelter from the elements while they traveled. As settlers began to expand westward, they discovered that the limestone cavern system had a very large supply of saltpeter, a necessary ingredient in gunpowder. The saltpeter was so abundant that Union soldiers built an on-site munitions plant to supply troops with gunpowder.

In addition, in 1874, the caves were a known hideout for Jesse James, who also happens to turn up in the chapter on Kansas. James was known to hide in these caves for days at a time between his robberies. One of the ghosts associated with Meramec Caverns is rumored to be that of Jesse James himself.

At the end of the nineteenth century, the caverns were used by Missouri's wealthy to host gala parties, including formal balls.

Since the Meramec Caverns opened to the public in the 1930s, there have been several sightings of ghosts throughout the caves.

The oldest ghost at the Meramec Caverns is that of a Native American woman who is often seen standing in a pool of water quite a distance away from the marked path that leads tourists to the lower levels. Whether she drowned in one of the pools or some other fate befell her at the caverns is unknown.

Another ghost is that of a woman in a formal dress who is seen near one of the larger formations called the Pendulum. As she is described as wearing a formal dress, the ghost is likely a woman who attended one of the many underground balls that were held in the large, open caverns.

A third ghost is referred to by locals simply as the Man in Black. This lone, shadowy figure has often been seen watching the visitors on the tours from afar. He appears so real that sometimes a tourist will ask their guide why they left one of the group behind. The identity of this man in black is not known, but speculations as to who this mystery man is have ranged from Jesse James to Lester Dill.

Harney Mansion
332 South Mansion Street

The Harney Mansion was originally built as a private residence by Dr. Alson Laffingwell in 1856. General William S. Harney purchased the mansion and the surrounding 1,900 acres in 1872. Soon after the purchase was finalized, Harney made some considerable modifications to the main house, including having an exact duplicate of the original mansion added to the original structure. Once it was completed, General Harney used the property as a summer house for several years. Finally, in 1884, Harney moved to Florida permanently, where he died on May 9, 1889.

Early in his military career, Harney developed a reputation for being a very strict and often brutal man. During the Battle of Ash Hollow in 1855, he was said to be responsible in the deaths of over eighty-five men, women, and children. In St. Louis, he was tried and acquitted of the beating death of Hanna, one of his slaves, for apparently losing his keys. Although he seemed to have a violent streak early in life, later on Harney became well-known as a very fair and diplomatic negotiator between the Native Americans and the American settlers. He was so good at negotiating and mediating that after his death he became known as "Man-who-keeps-his-word" among the Crow Indian tribe.

Several reports of paranormal activity have been associated with the mansion, most of which started in the 1980s after renovations to preserve the mansion began. Bright lights have been seen throughout the house, although when many of these were encountered, the mansion had no electricity on at the time. It is also common to notice various aromas throughout the mansion, the most prevalent being the smell of pipe tobacco smoke.

Over the years, apparitions have also been reported at the Harney Mansion. The apparition of a middle-aged man that has an uncanny resemblance to a photograph of General Harney has been seen throughout the mansion. Another apparition is that of a small woman who is seen walking in the main hallways and the dining area. An interesting aspect of these apparitions is that General Harney's apparition always appears very clear, the woman's ghost is more hazy and blurred. It is possible that the female ghost is that of Hanna, the slave girl that General Harney was accused of killing.

Waynesville

·························

Phantom Rider

Robbidoux Creek

The story of the Phantom Rider of Pulaski County has been a well-known local legend in the Waynesville area for generations. Most versions are very similar and begin when a Confederate colonel by the name of Charles Potter moved to the area after his wife had been killed by Union soldiers. By most accounts, Charles Potter was a fairly mild-mannered man who simply wanted to move on from the ravages of the Civil War and be left alone. However, that was not going to be the case.

It so happened that there was a preacher by the name of Elder Maupins who lived near Springfield. Elder Maupins had been said to be living a double life. During the day, he was a well-respected preacher of a small church near Springfield. However, at night, Maupins was the leader of a group of criminals that eventually became known as Maupins's Marauders or Maupins's Raiders. This band of outlaws had been known to terrorize the citizens of Springfield, Waynesville, and surrounding areas. For quite some time, most people were oblivious that the man who had robbed so many people was, in actuality, a preacher.

No one knows how many people knew that the preacher was the leader of the Marauders, but the knowledge did spread. Eventually, Colonel Potter found out what Elder Maupins was doing and decided to confront him. Knowing that Maupins would be at the church during a Sunday service, Colonel Potter entered the church on horseback and confronted him in the presence of the entire church congregation. Colonel Potter called Elder Maupins out on his criminal activity and drew his sword in order to kill the preacher. Before he was able to kill Maupins, Colonel Potter was fatally shot by Teddy Jergans, a member of the congregation and Maupins's second-in-command of the Marauders. The gunshot that killed Potter spooked his horse, which bolted from the church and was never seen again. According to some versions of the tale, the horse ran from the church with Potter's body lying lifeless on its back. However, others claim that Potter was thrown from the horse when it was startled and that Maupin continued his church service with the lifeless body of Colonel Potter still lying next to the altar.

Shortly after the death of Colonel Potter, parishioners started to distance themselves from Elder Maupin and his church. Within a few weeks of Potter's death, residents started to tell stories of seeing a large glowing light near the church. People started to drift away from going to Maupins's church services. This gave Maupins more time to rob and terrorize the residents. With nobody attending his church, Maupin turned the church into a base of operations from which to plan his attacks and robberies.

Although his lawbreaking increased, Maupins's crime spree was very short-lived. One night, Maupins and Jergans were apparently killed, their bodies were found along the road near the church. Although it is uncertain how Jergans died, Elder Maupins was decapitated by a sharp object. Remembering that Colonel Potter drew his sword during the church service, most people believed that Potter had come back from the dead to exact his revenge against Maupins and Jergans.

To this day, there are accounts by people who have gone where the church used to stand that they can hear a horse snorting and whinnying. In addition, near the site where the bodies of Maupins and Jergans were found, bright bluish-white lights ranging in size from a softball to a basketball have been reported. When approached, the lights will fly away. Sometimes a whinny and a gallop from a phantom horse can be heard just before the lights disappear.

The church is said to still be standing, although it is in ruins from lack of upkeep. It is located in Pulaski County about two miles west of the Robbidoux Creek area, which is about four miles north of downtown Waynesville, Missouri.

Springfield

....

Pythian Castle (Orphanage)
1451 East Pythian Street

The Pythian Castle was built in 1913 by the Knights of Pythias, which was a fraternal organization that had a chapter in Springfield, Missouri. The Knights of Pythias was founded in 1864 as a fraternal brotherhood, similar to the Freemasons, that focused on loyalty, friendship, and honor. Today, there are over 50,000 members and over 2,000 lodges throughout the world. Some of the larger lodges have built Pythian Castles, which have been known to help orphans and the widows of the Knights of Pythians who have already passed on.

In Springfield, Missouri, the Pythian Castle was intentionally built to resemble a castle so that it could be a standing testament to what the Knights of Pythias represented. Originally, the Pythian Castle was built as an orphanage for children and a retirement home for the widows of members of the Knights of Pythias. It also served as a grand meeting lodge for local members of the Knights of Pythias.

The role of the castle as an orphanage and meeting lodge remained unchanged from 1913 until 1942. When World War II broke out, the United States government took control of both the Pythian Castle and nearby O'Reiley Hospital to care for wounded American GIs coming home from war. While the O'Reiley Hospital focused on tending to the primary medical needs of the injured soldiers, the Pythian Castle primarily offered rehabilitation and entertainment opportunities for the soldiers once they were released from the hospital. The castle provided several amenities for the soldiers such as a bowling alley, a movie theater, a ballroom, a pool hall, and a library. In addition, several great entertainers from the 1940s made unannounced visits to the soldiers.

After World War II ended, the castle was abandoned for a few years and was finally sold to a private individual who renovated it and has recently opened it as a community cultural arts and events center.

Since before World War II, the Pythian Castle had the reputation for being haunted by the ghosts of children who lived at the orphanage. The disembodied voices of children playing, laughing, or crying have been heard throughout the castle. Several of these voices have been recorded as EVPs (electronic voice phenomenon) by amateur and professional ghost hunters who have investigated the castle. Photographs of ghost children have also been taken over the years on those same ghost hunts.

There have also been reports of adult voices heard throughout the Pythian Castle. These voices simply appear to be in conversation and are likely the residual energy of the soldiers who stayed at the castle during their rehabilitation after being released from nearby O'Reiley Hospital. Whether it be the ghosts of children or adults, most of the ghosts at the Pythian Castle are fairly benign.

One ghost encountered on the fifth floor of the castle is that of a large man who once worked at the orphanage. Rumor had it that he was very abusive to the children at the orphanage and threatened them with more severe abuse, or even death, if they would ever tell anybody what happened. When this spirit is encountered, people will often describe a very strong sense of anger or oppression coming from the ghost.

Pythian Castle has had such a reputation for being haunted that it has been the subject of several books, at least one documentary, and has even been the focus of the Discovery Channel's *Ghost Labs* in 2011. The castle has been confirmed haunted by the Ozark Paranormal Society and the Paranormal Task Force. Today, the castle offers ghost tours and ghost hunts on a regular basis.

Joe's Cave

According to local legend, in 1836, a slave named Joe lived with the Daniel Fulbright family in the Waynesburg area. Not a lot is known about Joe other than that he was trusted by the Fulbrights and that he could play the fiddle better than almost anybody in the entire county. Joe's reputation with the fiddle was such that he would often be asked to play at parties and other gatherings on a regular basis.

One day, Joe had been asked by Mr. Fulbright and his daughter, Amanda, to help out with some projects in the farmhouse. Not foreseeing any problems, Mr. Fulbright left Joe and Amanda alone together while he went to town to run some errands.

Not long after Mr. Fulbright left, Joe and Amanda got into an argument. In a fit of rage, Joe stabbed Amanda in the chest with a knife. Amanda left the house, bleeding profusely and yelling loudly in pain. Fearful that somebody would hear her, Joe panicked and strangled Amanda Fulbright to death in the yard near the house. Looking at Amanda's lifeless body in the yard and the blood on his own hands, Joe knew what would become of him if he was caught by Mr. Fulbright. In order to save himself, Joe ran into the woods.

Once Daniel Fulbright discovered the strangled body of his daughter and that Joe was nowhere to be found, he knew that Joe was the murderer. Fulbright formed a posse to bring the killer to justice. After hours of searching, Joe was eventually found near a series of caves not far from Fulbright's farm. Although Joe was cornered by the posse, he attempted to run deeper into the caves. A man by the name of Raferty shot Joe and mortally wounded him. Fulbright ordered that a doctor be called to tend to Joe's gunshot wound. However, due to the severity of the injury, Joe died shortly after the doctor arrived.

After Joe died, Fulbright refused to allow him to be buried anywhere near his daughter or the family grave plots. Apparently, slaves throughout the area had the same sentiment, and they pleaded that Joe not be buried in one of their cemeteries fearing that it would become cursed. The landowners heeded their requests and refused to allow Joe to be buried on their land.

A few days had passed since Joe had been killed, and something needed to be done with his rapidly decaying body. The doctor who had attempted to treat Joe came up with an idea. He requested to take custody of Joe's body from Fulbright for medical study. The doctor explained that it gave him a specimen to work with and solved the problem with what to do with the body since it was apparent that nobody wanted Joe in their cemeteries.

Joe's body was moved into a small cave near the doctor's residence. Once there, the doctor began to dissect the corpse, careful to take meticulous notes on the condition of Joe's overall health at the time of death and anything else that may have interested him. While the doctor's request to move Joe's body to a cave may have seemed rather odd, it made perfect sense. The cave was private and isolated. It was not near the doctor's home and very few people knew of its location. Also, the coolness of the cave helped to slow decomposition. This gave the doctor additional time to study Joe's remains in detail without distraction.

Once the doctor's study of the specimen was complete, he cut the body into smaller pieces, careful not to scrape any of the bones. He then boiled these parts until the flesh easily fell clean from the bones. The bones were wired together into a complete skeleton and moved to a local university where it was placed in a classroom. When asked, the doctor never revealed where he acquired the skeleton.

The story of Joe does not end there. Not long after his body was taken to the classroom, he started to make his presence known. Students began to talk about hearing a fiddle playing in the room where the skeleton was kept. People who were privy to the location of the caves were where Joe was shot also claim to have heard fiddle music playing from within the mouth of the cave ever since Joe died. Finally, for years after Joe's death, the same fiddle music was heard at the Fulbright residence usually close to the anniversary of Amanda's death.

As a final note, one year, Joe's skeleton disappeared from the classroom and what became of it is unknown. Some say that it is still at the medical school in storage. Others say that the doctor's descendants or students learned of the skeleton's true origins and took it back to one of the caves near where his murder took place.

Landers Theatre/Springfield Little Theatre
311 East Walnut Street

Built in 1909, the Landers Theatre was the major venue of live entertainment for people in and around Springfield, Missouri. From 1909 until 1920, the Landers Theatre was famous for having some of the best names in show business perform on stage, including John Philip Sousa, Lon Chaney, and the Weaver Brothers. Today, after the Springfield Little Theatre Organization purchased the Landers in 1970 and completed considerable renovations before reopening, it is now known as the Springfield Little Theatre. The 641-seat theater has approximately 50,000 to 60,000 visitors for their theatrical and musical performances each year.

There are ghosts that are believed to haunt the Springfield Little Theatre. These wayward spirits include a heroic janitor, a crying baby and her distraught mother, and a stage manager.

On December 18, 1920, there was a fire in the Landers. A janitor happened to be working when the fire broke out. Through his actions, the theater was saved from total destruction, but he died from smoke inhalation and severe burns over much of his body. Today, there is a section of the theater that sometimes smells of thick, heavy smoke. This smell is often accompanied by the apparition of a man who appears to be desperately trying to put out a fire with a jacket or blanket. When he is approached, both the apparition and the smell will disappear.

Although the theater was saved by the janitor, damages were extensive enough to keep the theater closed for several months. After considerable repairs, the Landers Theater reopened for business on May 21, 1921.

Not long after this section of the theater was reopened, a young mother brought her sleeping baby into a matinee show. She went to the balcony of the theater so they wouldn't disturb the people in the auditorium below.

The baby woke up and started to cry. In an attempt to quiet the baby, the woman got up and started to quietly sing a lullaby. Unfortunately, she slipped and the baby fell over the edge of the balcony to the ground several feet below. Although the mother and several bystanders tried to revive the infant, nothing could be done and the baby died from broken bones and internal bleeding.

Today, a baby crying frantically can be heard in the balcony, especially if a rehearsal is being done on stage. The crying is usually followed by the soft sound of a mother's voice trying to comfort the baby. Sometimes a lullaby can even be made out. A handful of people over the years have claimws to have seen a young woman holding a baby watching the performance from the balcony.

Another ghost is known to haunt an area backstage. A stage manager allegedly committed suicide backstage after a show's final performance. He waited until the rest of the people left for the night and hanged himself. His body was not discovered until the next day. The stage manager was well liked and pleasant, and his decision to commit suicide was unexpected by everybody who knew him. Today, there is a section near where the man's body was found that is usually much colder than any other part of the theater. Also, an apparition of the man will appear. When the apparition appears, it is usually followed by severe electrical problems with lighting and other equipment.

Joplin

Peace Church Cemetery
Peace Church Avenue

The body of one of the most notorious spree killers of the 1950s, William Cook Jr., is buried in an unmarked grave in Peace Church Cemetery located in Joplin, Missouri. The story of Billy Cook is indeed a sad story that starts, and ultimately ends, in Joplin.

William "Billy" Cook Jr. was born on December 23, 1928, in a small shack near Joplin. There, he lived with his mother, father, and seven brothers and sisters in abject poverty. Billy's mother died when he was only five years old, and soon Billy's father, William Cook Sr., was unable to keep the shack that they were living in. Billy's father, being a mine-worker with little formal education and few friends, moved the entire family into an abandoned mine shaft near Joplin.

It is uncertain how long Billy's father kept them alone in the mine-shaft with few clothes and even fewer supplies. However, one night, Billy's father went into town and got drunk at a local bar. After leaving the bar several hours later, William Cook Sr. hopped on a boxcar train and left town. Several days passed before authorities found Billy Cook and his abandoned brothers and sisters. With no family available to take care of the children, they became wards of the state. Soon, all of the Cook children, with the exception of Billy, were placed with foster parents in the area. Finally, a woman took Billy in, but it was obvious that she was more interested in the money she would receive from the state rather than the welfare of the child.

Billy Cook eventually went to reform school because of truancy problems and continually getting into trouble with authority figures. Cook was unable to finish school and, due to his violent streak and inability to conform to societal norms, he was sent to Missouri State Penitentiary when he was seventeen years old.

In 1950, Cook finished his sentence but was unable to find work that lasted more than a few weeks. He eventually purchased a .32 caliber pistol in El Paso, Texas. Shortly after buying the pistol, Cook kidnapped an auto mechanic and stole the man's vehicle. Cook ordered the mechanic into the trunk of the car and started to drive toward Oklahoma City. Luckily, the mechanic escaped from the trunk without Cook's knowledge. Cook only discovered this when the car ran out of gas several miles away.

Desperate to get back on the road, Cook abandoned the car and started to hitchhike to Oklahoma City. He was picked up by Carl Mosser and his family who were traveling on vacation. Cook murdered the entire family and dumped their bodies in a mineshaft on the outskirts of Joplin. The car was found blood-stained and full of bullet holes in Tulsa, Oklahoma. Police found the receipt for the gun Cook had purchased inside the car.

Cook's killing spree spanned several states and took the lives of seven people, including the Mossers. His victims included Carl Mosser (33), Thelma Mosser (29), Ronald Mosser (7), Gary Mosser (5), Pamela Mosser (3), Robert Dewey (32), and Homer Walldrip (he survived the shooting).

After several weeks on the run, Cook was finally found and arrested in Santa Rosalia, Mexico. He was extradited back to Oklahoma City to answer for the murders of the Mosser family. The judge sentenced him to 300 years in prison, but not the death penalty. After the conviction in Oklahoma, Cook was again extradited to California for the murder of Robert Dewey. For Dewey's murder, Cook was given the death penalty. He was executed in the gas chamber in San Quentin on December 12, 1952.

Being the next of kin, William Cook Sr. agreed to make funeral arrangements for his son. He contacted an undertaker by the name of Glen Boydston in Commanche, Oklahoma, who agreed to help him by embalming and burying his son. However, Boydston wanted to make a quick buck, so he put Cook's body on display and charged curious onlookers to see the body of the spree killer.

When Billy's father discovered this, he demanded that his son's body be moved back to Joplin, Missouri, for a proper burial. Due to the heinousness of the murders that Billy Cook committed, it was next to impossible to find a cemetery that would take his body. Finally, it was agreed that Cook's body could be laid to rest at the Peace Church Cemetery with certain conditions. The grave had to be unmarked and separate from the rest of the cemetery. William Cook Sr. agreed to this. A grave was dug and a midnight graveside service was conducted by flashlight and lantern by Reverend Dow Booe. Other than the reverend, the only person in attendance at the service was Billy's father.

Since Billy Cook was buried, there are those who believe that his ghost haunts the Peace Church Cemetery. Late at night, there have been reports of a group of lights seen near the far edge of the cemetery. It could very likely be that these lights are actually the lanterns that were held during the graveside service that Reverend Booe conducted for Billy Cook. There has also been a vaporous figure seen floating near an unmarked grave and wandering through the rest of the cemetery. People who have gone to the cemetery have also claimed to have seen a man standing at the tree line looking at them from the shadows with anger and hatred in his eyes.

THREE

KANSAS

---

13 miles

K ansas only has the bragging rights to a little over thirteen of the 2,448 miles of Route 66. To put things into perspective, if a person was driving straight through Kansas on Route 66, it would take less than half an hour. However, there is a lot of history associated with this section of the state.

There were only a few ghost stories associated with the towns that Route 66 passed through directly. Rather than share accounts of a very few ghost stories for Kansas, I decided to expand my search to include stories in locations within a two-hour drive of Galena, which is one of the towns along the thirteen-mile stretch of Route 66 that passes through Kansas.

Galena

Galena

....

Galena is a peaceful little town of a little over three thousand residents. Simply driving through the town today does not give a person a true feel of Galena's rich history. Just like the miners who helped to put this town on the map in the nineteenth century, a person will have to dig much deeper to discover more about the historical significance of this small town.

Prior to 1877, the area was known mostly to Native American tribes, hunters and trappers, and the occasional outlaw trying to escape from justice. Although the Native Americans knew of the lead for years, in the spring of 1877 two men discovered a large untapped vein of lead ore. Word soon spread and by June of that year, two rival mining companies, the Galena Mining and Smelting Company and the South Side Town and Mining Company, came to the area. The two companies formed separate camps that soon grew into two towns—Empire City and Galena. Because both companies wanted the same resource, a bitter rivalry between the two businesses started over the mining rights.

Red Hot Street

The rivalry between Empire City and Galena escalated to the point that the road that connected the two towns became known as Red Hot Street. Shortly after the towns were formed, saloons, brothels, and gambling establishments were quickly built along Red Hot Street to accommodate the three thousand miners that the two mining companies had employed. If a lead miner wanted to lose his hard-earned money or his life, Red Hot Street was the place to do it. Fights, robberies, and murders were not uncommon in this part of town. In order to take advantage of this macabre opportunity, some undertakers and doctors were open only at night to better accommodate their clientele.

After the mining companies stopped producing the lead ore in the 1970s, Galena's population eventually decreased considerably. Some of the original buildings still stand as a testament to its rich mining history.

Although Galena is not nearly as bustling as it once was, a person does not have to travel very far to see that it did provide a varied history... a history that undoubtedly has produced its fair share of ghost stories and paranormal experiences.

Schermerhorn Park
3501 S Main Street

Less than three miles from downtown Galena is a place called Schermerhorn Park. Deep within the park's acreage is a 2,500-foot deep cave that is reported to have been one of the many hiding places of the famous outlaw Jesse James. Over the years, people who have gone into the cave claimed that they could hear men talking and an occasional gunshot. However, upon further investigation, the cave was always empty.

Jesse James and his band of outlaws traveled through Galena on more than one occasion. According to accounts from Galena's newspaper, a man by the name of George Shepherd traveled there to announce that he actually had a shootout with Jesse James and had killed him.

Oak Hill Cemetery
Columbus Street

The Oak Hill Cemetery dates back to the mid-1800s, shortly before Galena first experienced its population explosion due to the zinc and lead mining companies that arrived there in 1877. Several accounts of paranormal activity at the cemetery date back to at least the early 1900s.

The old Oak Hill Cemetery was also known as the Empire City Cemetery in the late 1800s because it was closer to the Empire City section of Red Hot Street. Several of the miners who met their untimely deaths on Red Hot Street were taken to the Oak Hill Cemetery because of its proximity.

One ghost story associated with Oak Hill Cemetery is of a woman accused of being a witch who was buried in the wooded area toward the back of the graveyard. Locals would sneak into this section of the cemetery late at night to try to catch a glimpse of the Witch of Oak Hill Cemetery. As one approaches the rear of the cemetery, a lone grave marker can be found. Strange sounds like mumbling or chanting have been heard. Also, people have seen a figure walking near the gravesite. As this apparition approaches a nearby tree, it disappears. Some speculate that something valuable or important is buried there.

Another account that pertains to the Oak Hill Cemetery concerns a man who did not give his wife a proper funeral when she died unexpectedly. He arranged to have her buried in the crudest, cheapest coffin available and was miserly when it came to the funeral itself. A few days after she was buried, the gravestone cracked. The widower replaced the gravestone and within a few days, it also cracked. The man attempted to replace the gravestone a few more times, and each time the same thing happened. Eventually, the man gave up on trying to replace the gravestone and moved away.

In addition to the gravestone and the reports of the witch in the back of the cemetery, dozens of people who have visited the cemetery have felt a very strong presence toward the center of the cemetery. This is where the people who died along Red Hot Street were buried.

Baxter Springs
(less than ten minutes from Route 66)

Fort Baxter

Camp Baxter was originally constructed in the early months of 1862. Originally, the camp was to act as a garrison for Union soldiers who traveled through the area from one fort to another in the days immediately after the South seceded from the United States in 1861. Nearly 5,000 Union troops had stayed at Camp Baxter at one time or another. Eventually, several other camps were constructed nearby.

The following year, with the number of Union troops steadily passing through the area, it was decided that Camp Baxter would be the perfect site for a permanent fort. So Camp Baxter was dismantled and Fort Blair was built. Although officially named Fort Blair, some continued to refer to it as Fort Baxter. Another fort built within a day's ride of Fort Blair was Fort Scott, which was about sixty miles to the north.

Not long after Fort Blair was constructed in 1863, Confederate guerrilla William Quantrill and his band of Quantrill's Raiders decided to attack. On October 6, 1863, a group of several hundred of Quantrill's Raiders divided into two separate groups and attempted a surprise attack on Fort Blair. Quantrill and his men had been responsible for the destruction of Lawrence, Kansas, just a few months before, so the soldiers at Fort Blair were well aware of Quantrill's activities. Although Quantrill had close to four hundred men in his band of guerilla fighters, he was unable to take Fort Blair. Pushed back by the Union forces inside the fort, Quantrill ordered his men to retreat.

After retreating from their failed attack on Fort Blair, Quantrill and his Raiders met up with a Union detachment that was escorting Major General James Blunt from nearby Fort Scott to Fort Smith in Arkansas. The outnumbered Union soldiers were taken entirely by surprise. By the time the ambush was over, most of the one hundred Union soldiers had been killed. A few survivors escaped to the safety of Fort Scott. By the time reinforcements from Fort Scott arrived to the scene, Quantrill and his men had already fled the area.

Once it was confirmed that Quantrill was not waiting for another ambush, the new task at hand was to retrieve the bodies of the soldiers who had been killed in what would be known as either the Battle of Fort Blair or the Fort Baxter Massacre. Because of the proximity and the number of bodies that needed to be recovered, they were taken to Fort Blair.

After all of the bodies were gathered inside the fort, they were given a funeral and buried in a makeshift graveyard near the fort.

Shortly after the massacre, it was decided that Fort Blair was no longer an asset to the Union Army and was ordered to be decommissioned. The soldiers who had been stationed at Fort Blair were permanently reassigned and the final few men who stayed behind burned the fort to the ground to prevent it from getting into enemy hands.

As soon as the Civil War ended in April 1865, people were starting to settle in the area near where the fort had stood. Now that the acreage that had been the site of Fort Blair was cleared, it was the prime location for settlers to build their homes and farms. Within a few years after the Civil War, the land that contained both Fort Blair and the cemetery had new homes built on it.

Many of the settlers did not realize that they had built on land over the bodies of nearly one hundred Union soldiers, but they soon found out that something definitely was not right. Shortly after people began moving into their homes, the settlers started to notice uniformed Union soldiers walking outside of their homes. This was rather a peculiar sight, since the war had been over for months. When the owners investigated, they could not find anybody nearby. On some occasions, people were startled to see the soldiers standing over their beds late at night.

Although most of the ghostly activity was in the form of apparitions of soldiers walking in and near their homes, settlers would occasionally hear a soldier cry out in pain or a gunshot that had no known source.

In 1885, Congress approved creating a national cemetery for the soldiers who died in the Battle of Fort Blair. The land was purchased from the settlers and the bodies were exhumed and reburied in a proper military cemetery about a mile from the original makeshift graveyard. The original site of Fort Blair and the cemetery was made into a state park commemorating the fort. To this day, people can still see the Union soldiers walking in the area where Fort Blair once stood.

Columbus
(approximately 30 minutes from Route 66)
....

Spooksville Triangle

Much like the lights that have been seen around Joplin, Missouri, the "spook lights" of the Columbus, Kansas, area have become the stuff of local legend. There have been so many sightings of the luminescent orbs over the years that the area between Columbus, Kansas, Miami, Oklahoma, and Joplin, Missouri, has been dubbed the Spooksville Triangle.

The spook lights have been documented in the area for well over 125 years. The first written account of the spook lights can be found in an article written by Foster Young entitled "The Ozark Spook Light," which was printed in 1881. The article describes the lights pretty much as they are seen today, which would cast doubt onto the theory that the lights are actually the reflection of headlights from nearby roads or flashlights from hikers. Although the definitive source for the spook lights is uncertain, several legends have attempted to explain how they came into existence.

One legend goes that a young the daughter of a Cherokee chief wanted to marry a warrior from another tribe, but her father refused to allow the marriage to take place. Rather than abide by her father's wishes, the young couple ran away together. When her father learned of this, he sent several of his finest warriors to find his daughter and her lover to bring them both back to his village. In typical Thelma and Louise tradition, the young lovers opted to leap to their deaths into nearby Spring River (not far from Baxter Springs) rather than to be captured by their pursuers. According to this legend, the lights are the spirits of the two lovers and the warriors who are searching for all eternity. A variation of this legend is that the lovers did not kill themselves, but the chief's daughter agreed not to see her paramour again. However, she soon died of a broken heart and the spook light is her ghost trying to find the man she loved.

A second legend is that a miner returned home from several days of mining in the hills near Galena only to find that while he was working, his cabin had been attacked. He was a quiet, God-fearing family man who worked hard to help support his wife and young child. He searched through the ruins of the cabin and the surrounding area, but his family was nowhere to be found. According to this legend, the spook light is actually the ghost of the miner who is searching the area for his wife and child with a lantern.

Another legend that attempts to explain the spook lights is associated with none other than William Quantrill, infamous leader of the a band of several hundred rogues known to use guerrilla-type tactics that led to the deaths of several hundred men, women, and children in this area. Quantrill was known to frequent this area when not attacking others. The lights could be the ghost of Quantrill being chased by several of his victims.

Coffeyville
(approximately 1.25 hours from Route 66)
....

Brown Mansion
2019 South Walnut

Built in 1904, the Brown Mansion in Coffeyville, Kansas, was named after businessman W. P. Brown, who made a considerable fortune in the lumber and natural gas industries. After meeting his future wife, Nancy, in Independence, Kansas, the couple moved to her hometown of Port Washington, Ohio, but eventually returned to the Coffeyville area to start a family in the 1880s.

Although W. P. and Nancy Brown did have five children, only one lived into adulthood. The Browns had two sons who died at birth, one son that died when he was four years old of pneumonia, and one son who died at the age of eleven of complications due to diabetes. Their only daughter, Violet, left home and married at the age of nineteen. As she grew up in Coffeyville prior to the Brown Mansion being built in 1904, she never spent any of her childhood in the mansion.

According to the official website, the three-story, sixteen-room Brown Mansion was constructed in 1904 at a cost of $125,000. The first floor had a formal dining area, a library, a billiards room, and a solarium to entertain the many guests that they received on a regular basis. The second floor included five bedrooms and three full baths, which was quite a luxury in the early 1900s. The mansion's third floor had a gigantic open ballroom that also served as a classroom and play area for their son Donald, who was the only one of the Brown children who lived at the mansion. Rather than go to a private or public school, Donald's parents made certain that he was homeschooled by private tutors and Mrs. Brown herself.

Donald apparently had some severe health problems and died of complications to his diabetes in 1910 when he was only eleven years old. Mrs. Brown was so grief-stricken after Donald died that she arranged to have his bedroom on the second floor sealed off—with strict orders never to open it again under any circumstances.

Several years after her brother's death, Violet returned to Coffeyville and the Brown Mansion in order to help take care of her elderly and ailing parents. In the little free time that she had from being her parents' caretaker, Violet could be found dancing in the ballroom on the third floor.

Shortly after her mother's death in 1937, Violet arranged to have Donald's room reopened. It was the first time in twenty-six years that the room had been used. Violet felt that enough time had passed and that they should move on. She did not open the room earlier out of respect for her mother's wishes. After her father died, Violet inherited the mansion in 1970 and decided to sell the mansion to the Coffeyville Historical Society.

There are accounts of at least five ghosts that haunt Brown Mansion today, the most active of which is that of W. P. Brown himself. He is usually seen sitting in the first-floor dining room or library smoking a pipe. Occasionally, the smell of pipe tobacco can be noticed in these rooms.

Mrs. Brown is one of the other ghosts believed to haunt Brown Mansion. She is usually found outside of her son Donald's bedroom crying, which is heard much more often than her apparition, which has been seen infrequently.

Donald Brown is also said to haunt Brown Mansion. His ghost is sometimes seen in his bedroom as well as on the third floor where he was homeschooled. Unlike his mother's ghost, Donald's ghost appears to be much happier and carefree. His apparition is most often seen on the third floor, where he can be heard whistling one of his favorite songs.

Violet's ghost has been seen in the third-floor ballroom, where she spent much of her free time when she was not actively taking care of her parents. When Violet's ghost is witnessed on the third floor, she is seen dancing, apparently oblivious to the fact that it has been nearly forty years since she died in 1973.

The final ghost that is known to haunt Brown Mansion is a servant by the name of Charlie. Not a lot is known about Charlie other than the fact that he was well respected by the Browns to the point of being considered a member of the family. The servants at Brown Mansion had separate living quarters on the basement level, which also contained a wine cellar, a laundry, and storage rooms. Charlie can be seen sitting in his room in the basement or standing by the front entrance as if he is waiting to open the door for guests.

Beaumont
(approximately 2.5 hours from Route 66)

The Beaumont Hotel
11651 SE Main Street

The Beaumont Hotel opened its doors in 1879 as a cozy little respite for those who were weary from long hours of riding the stagecoach trails and railroads from the east. The Beaumont was an oasis in an otherwise inhospitable and often dangerous environment.

This hotel was the brainchild of a married couple by the name of Edwin and Emma Russell, who originally named it the Summit Hotel from 1879 until 1885, when the hotel was renamed the Beaumont Hotel. Shortly after opening, people would sometimes go out of their way to make a stop at this hotel. It offered warm, clean beds, a hot bath, a home-cooked meal, and personal hospitality that was second to none. Perhaps another reason travelers would stop at the Beaumont is that it also served as a part-time brothel.

According to some accounts, Mr. Russell made a rather unique and lucrative business proposition with his wife. While he took care of the legitimate business dealings associated with running the hotel, she would meet travel-weary and often wealthy traveling businessmen in their room for a discreet rendezvous.

It just so happened that one of Emma's regular customers was a young cowboy named Zeke. As hard as he tried not to, Zeke fell in love with Emma. Apparently, she had similar feelings, and the two started having an affair. She stopped charging Zeke for her services and the two would often meet in secret and were making plans of running away together one day.

Eventually, Edwin Russell discovered the affair and confronted Zeke in the room where he sometimes met with his lover. The two men started to argue loudly. When Zeke professed his love for Emma, Edwin became even more enraged and tried to attack Zeke. The fight escalated to the point that Zeke pulled his gun on the hotel owner. However, Edwin was too quick and fired first. He shot Zeke dead in the very same room where the cowboy had been sleeping with his wife for the past several months.

Over the years, the Beaumont Hotel has changed hands several times, but has remained open for over 133 years. Although the hotel is just as busy today, it is partly because it caters to people who want an opportunity to catch a glimpse of Zeke, who has haunted the hotel since the day he was gunned down.

Zeke makes his presence known in his room at the Beaumont Hotel in several different ways. Sometimes, guests will awaken to find that a chair was placed against the doorknob of the room door so that nobody can enter the room.

It has also been said that, in several rooms, clock radios that have not had an alarm set will sometimes have their alarm go off between 2:00 a.m. and 3:00 a.m. on certain nights. This has been known to happen in rooms that were vacant at the time the alarm went off. It is believed that this is the time that Zeke was shot and killed by the hotel owner.

Several guests at the Beaumont Hotel have been awakened by a loud banging sound outside of their doors late at night. Others have heard the loud sound of cowboy boots with spurs walking back and forth in front of their doors. Some have even claimed to have seen the apparition of a young cowboy standing at the top of a set of stairs. However, when people investigate, there is no sign that anybody was in the stairway.

In addition to the haunting, the Beaumont Hotel is unique in one other aspect. For nearly sixty years, it has been a favorite stop for many private airplane pilots in the area. The hotel and restaurant has a personal grass runway where pilots can land their planes in safety to take in the scenic vista, have a good meal, or try to find the ghost of a cowboy named Zeke.

Lawrence
(approximately 3 hours from Route 66)

....

Eldridge Hotel
701 Massachusetts Street

The Eldridge (photo courtesy Nancy Longhurst)

The original hotel on this site was built in 1855 and was known as the Free State Hotel. In the years prior to the Civil War, there was a great deal of racial tension in Kansas. Some residents felt that the state should secede to become a Confederate state while others believed that it should remain a free state.

The Free State Hotel was named as such because the owners wished to let people know their position on the slavery issue and their desire to see Kansas as a free state. In May 1856, less than a year after opening, the Free State Hotel was attacked by a large group of pro-slavery men who burned the hotel to the ground. The following year in 1857, Colonel

Sharlon Eldridge rebuilt the hotel at great personal expense. After it was constructed, he vowed that if any tyrants destroyed the hotel again, he would simply build a larger, more elaborate hotel on the same site.

Five years later in 1862, the hotel was once again destroyed, this time by William Quantrill and his group of renegades. Quantrill was intimately familiar with Lawrence, Kansas. In 1859 and 1860, Quantrill was actually a schoolteacher in that town. Having developed a reputation for being an alcoholic and a troublemaker, Quantrill eventually left Lawrence and went to Texas. There, he learned the basics of guerrilla fighting from Joel B. Mayes and joined the Cherokee Nation. Soon after, he joined the Confederate Army. However, he soon deserted from the Confederate Army and decided to start his own "army."

Within a fairly short time, Quantrill had amassed an organized group of nearly four hundred men to wage guerilla-type attacks on Union supporters, towns, forts, and soldiers. Due to the chaotic manner in which he conducted these attacks, many Confederate sympathizers did not approve of Quantrill. The men who followed Quantrill became known as Quantrill's Raiders. It should be noted that famous outlaw Jesse James was a member of Quantrill's Raiders when he was only sixteen years old. James stayed with Quantrill's Raiders until 1864.

On August 21, 1863, William Quantrill and his army descended upon the unsuspecting town of Lawrence. Quantrill was a diehard Confederate and did not like that the town of Lawrence had adopted such a pro-Union stance. As Quantrill had once lived in Lawrence, he was well aware of the promise that Eldridge made about the hotel, which may have factored into his decision to attack Lawrence. Within a matter of a few hours, the entire town of Lawrence, including the hotel, was literally burned to the ground. By the time the attack was over, nearly two hundred men and boys had been slaughtered and most of the surviving residents were homeless. These men were not only responsible for the destruction of Lawrence, Kansas, but also the attack on Fort Blair in Baxter Springs, Kansas.

Within a few days of Quantrill's attack, the surviving residents banded together, buried their dead, and began to rebuild the town. Colonel Eldridge kept to his word and rebuilt the hotel a second time in 1864. As a memorial to those who died and a reminder that people can overcome tragedy, Eldridge used one of the original cornerstones of the hotel that Quantrill had destroyed. When this hotel was opened, it was renamed the Eldridge Hotel.

With such a dramatic and turbulent history, there are several ghost stories associated with the Eldridge Hotel. Several floors are said to be haunted, but perhaps the hotel's most haunted area is the fifth floor, the top floor.

Room 506 is believed to be the most haunted. People staying in this room will experience doors opening and closing by themselves, the sound of heavy breathing, and mirrors fogging up as if somebody is breathing onto it. Most researchers who have investigated room 506 believe that the ghost is none other than Colonel Eldridge himself. The original cornerstone that Eldridge used from the destroyed hotel was placed in room 506, which may be why it has the highest concentration of ghostly activity. Although Eldridge did not die in the hotel, his apparition has been seen in the lobby smoking a pipe. A photograph was of a ghostly apparition was taken in an elevator that to this day has yet to be explained.

Sometimes, the elevator will malfunction. When a person hits the button for the basement, the elevator will often inexplicably take passengers to the fifth floor. When examined, there is never any mechanical problem found that could cause the malfunction. There have been sightings of the ghost of a man in his late teens or early twenties believed to be a former hotel employee. The apparition, always seen inside or near the elevator, has been photographed on several occasions. One of the most reproduced photos of the ghost in the elevator was taken during the Christmas holiday in 1989 and shows a shadowy figure standing inside the open elevator doors.

According to paranormal researchers who have investigated the Eldridge Hotel, besides the elevator and fifth floor, two other areas of the hotel are haunted. The first is the Crystal Ballroom. Inside this ballroom, for years people have heard voices speaking. Several EVPs have also been recorded by paranormal investigators in the Crystal Ballroom. Another area that has a high concentration of paranormal activity is the Big Six Room, which is located in the hotel's basement. In this room, a very high number of orbs have been photographed and EVPs recorded by paranormal investigators.

Kansas City
(approximately 3 hours from Route 66)

The Curious Case of Amantha Hatch

This peculiar story and obituary was originally published in the November 22, 1907, edition of the *Kansas City Journal*. Although not necessarily a ghost story associated with Route 66, it does warrant sharing. Besides, one of the best parts of Route 66 is that a person can take a detour at any time while traveling the Mother Road. Consider this story just that…a small detour.

Sometimes the veil between the living and the dead can become surprisingly thin. There have been many cases in which the severely ill and dying are provided glimpses of the afterlife and a foreknowledge of the date and details of their own demise. However, not so common are the stories of people who are in fairly good health who make a similar prediction.

Amantha Hatch was a fifty-eight-year-old wife and mother of two who lived in Peru, Kansas, about eighty miles west of Baxter Springs. Mrs. Hatch had traveled from Peru to Kansas City unexpectedly in order to visit her son, Dr. F. J. Hatch, and his family. At dinner one evening, Mrs. Hatch calmly said to her son, "Do you know I am going to die tonight?"

Dr. Hatch was naturally taken aback by Mrs. Hatch's statement. She was not the type of person to make odd or eccentric statements, and there was a sincerity in her voice that was a bit unsettling to Dr. Hatch. Had she been diagnosed with a terminal illness, it could be quite understandable for a person to make such a statement. However, Amantha Hatch was in good health and had no known medical conditions.

After dinner, Mrs. Hatch retired to her bedroom. She had requested that her son bring family photographs so that she could look at them. Her son did as he was asked and gathered up the photographs for his mother and closed the door behind him. There have been reports that Mrs. Hatch was heard speaking and laughing from behind the closed door as if she were holding a conversation with somebody. Perhaps she was.

While Mrs. Hatch was in the bedroom looking at the photographs, Dr. Hatch heard a knock at the front door. He answered it and a courier delivered a telegram that had been sent by his father. Mr. Hatch, Amantha's husband, sent a telegram to inform Dr. Hatch that he would be coming to Kansas City on the next train from Peru. He came shortly thereafter.

Later that evening, Dr. Hatch and his father were talking about the strange events that had recently transpired. According to Mr. Hatch, he had an overpowering urge to come to see his wife in Kansas City because he felt that her life was in danger.

Soon, Mrs. Hatch opened the bedroom door and asked to speak to both of her children and her husband individually. After saying her peace to each of them, she closed her eyes and died peacefully a short time later. Her son was quoted as saying, "She did not seem to die, but rather gain new life even up to the last. With a kind word for everyone upon her lips, she passed out of this life." Mrs. Hatch's body was returned to Peru, Kansas, the next day.

There have been no reported accounts of Mrs. Hatch's ghost being observed in either Kansas City or in Peru. However, there is little doubt that Mrs. Hatch definitely had a very uncanny sense of her untimely death.

FOUR

OKLAHOMA

---

432 miles

The 432 miles of Route 66 that passes through Oklahoma neatly cuts the state in half from the upper right corner to the lower left corner. As with much of Route 66, there are sections that have not been used commercially for years and are now nearly abandoned and forgotten. However, the spirit of Route 66 remains strong in Oklahoma. In many towns along the Mother Road, there are locations such as abandoned roads, theaters, and prisons where the spirits have been restless for years.

Miami
....

Coleman Theater
103 N. Main Street

The Coleman Theater was built by businessman George L. Coleman in 1928 at a cost of nearly $600,000, which, taking into

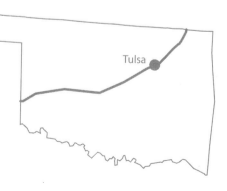

Tulsa

account interest, would be about $7,805,500 in today's dollars. His investment paid off greatly for both him and for the city of Miami, Oklahoma.

Shortly after it was opened on April 18, 1929, the Coleman Theater developed a very positive reputation for being a top-notch vaudeville theater, which attracted visitors and acts from all over the country and the world. Some of the entertainers who performed at the Coleman Theater include Will Rogers, Sally Rand, Bob Hope, Howard Keel, and Bing Crosby.

The four-level theater complex also included amenities such as two formal dining rooms, office space that could be rented, an art gallery, and various retail shops.

After being left vacant for several years, the Coleman Theater was added to the National Register of Historic Places in 1983. Today, people can arrange guided tours of the old theater, which has been restored in great detail down to the return of the original pipe organ, the "Mighty Wurlitzer," which was used during the theater's early days.

Based on eyewitness accounts over the years, there seems to be three ghosts associated with the Coleman Theater. The most prominent ghost is that of projection operator Mr. Roberts, who was the main projectionist until his death. During the time when movies were first becoming commonplace, working as a projectionist usually meant working in a cramped and hot projection room. Because of this, Mr. Roberts often wore strong bay rum cologne to cover up any perspiration. After his death, some people who have been given tours have noticed the smell of bay rum cologne in the projection room. Some have also claimed to have heard the sound of a man breathing heavily in the room.

According to local legend, the Coleman Theater was once the site of a mortuary. In the basement underneath the main seating area, there is a room that was the crematorium. Although it has not been used in this capacity for decades, there have been occasions when the room was extremely hot although there was no apparent source of the heat. Sometimes, a person whistling can be heard in this area.

The dressing rooms next to the main stage seem to be another hotbed of paranormal activity. People who have entered these rooms have reported noticing cold chills, the sound of indistinguishable voices, and an occasional apparition of a person getting ready to go on stage. It is not uncommon for electronic devices such as cameras and cellphones to lose all power here. Photos of orbs and misty forms have been taken in these rooms, particularly in the dressing room closest to the stage.

Claremore

Belvidere Mansion

121 North Chickasaw

The Belvidere Mansion was commissioned by wealthy investor and entrepreneur John Blayless in Claremore in 1902. John Blayless made his fortune by helping to create both the Arkansas and Oklahoma and the Cassville and Weston (C&W) railroads. Both railroads were crucial in the development of this part of Oklahoma and several other states and territories to the west.

John Blayless apparently believed that bigger was better. As he was one of the area's richest men, he decided that he should have a mansion that showed his wealth. Due to the size and detail of the mansion, it took more than five years to complete. A few of the features of the three-story, 9,000-square-foot mansion included having four distinct towers in a Gothic design, a 3,200-square-foot ballroom on the third floor to entertain guests, and many of the walls covered in pressed tin and marble—all of which were signs of prestige and affluence at the turn of the twentieth century. One unique feature of the mansion was that much of the wood used to decorate the interior was brought to Oklahoma from the 1904 World's Fair in St. Louis, Missouri.

Unfortunately, John Blayless would never live to see his mansion completed. Just six months before the mansion was scheduled to be finished, he developed appendicitis and died of complications from the surgery to remove his appendix. Rather than abandon the project, his wife, Mary

Melissa Blayless, took over and personally supervised the remainder of the mansion's construction and made certain that it met her late husband's expectations.

After the mansion was completed in late 1907, Mary Blayless and her seven children moved in and remained there for twelve more years until finally moving in 1919. After the Blayless family moved out, the building was sold a few times and eventually was converted into an apartment building in the 1930s and remained so until the 1960s. Eventually, the mansion went into disrepair and was in danger of being destroyed until it was purchased in 1991 by the Rogers County Historical Society, which is in the process of renovating it to Blayless's original condition.

There is little doubt that the Belvidere Mansion is haunted. Since renovations in the 1930s to convert the mansion into an apartment building, stories of ghosts have been told. Most of the paranormal activity in the Belvidere appears to take place on the second floor. In the living area, many people have claimed to have seen John Blayless and his wife Mary in several rooms on the second floor, particularly her bedroom. Specifically, misty forms have been photographed, and witnesses have reported seeing the apparition of both John and his wife. Also, throughout the mansion, people have heard the sound of children's laughter, although no children were around. John Blayless's ghost has also been seen on one of the porches by visitors touring the mansion.

Although most of the hauntings are associated with the Blayless family, there may be one ghost that has no ties to the original residents of the mansion. It has been said that during the 1940s, not long after the mansion had been converted into apartments, one of the residents became very depressed and, in an act of desperation, killed herself. There are those who say that you can hear a woman crying in the area that was her apartment. Sometimes this is accompanied by the apparition of a woman holding her face in her hands, crying.

As with several other hauntings of this type, there are typical electrical problems, cold spots, and the feelings of being watched.

Tulsa

....

Cain Ballroom

423 North Main Street

The internationally known and majestic Cain Dance Academy, later to be known as the Cain Ballroom, had very humble beginnings. After the building was constructed in 1924, it was used as a garage by Tate Brady, owner of the Brady Theater, which is described elsewhere in this chapter.

A few years after its construction, Brady arranged to make several renovations to the building, and it opened as a nightclub known as the Louvre. Brady noticed that several wealthy businessmen were coming to the area because of the oil and decided to open a place where they could relax and spend their money. This took place primarily during the Prohibition era. To bring customers in to the Louvre, big-name entertainers were booked and performed on a regular basis. Soon, the reputation of the Louvre began to spread, and people congregated to the nightclub just as much for the music as for the booze.

In 1930, the Louvre was sold to Madison Cain, who promptly changed the name of the establishment to Cain's Dance Academy. In addition to continuing to bring in some of the biggest names in show business, it also hosted several dances per week and even offered dance classes to those who wanted to learn how to cut a rug in style.

One of the regular acts at the Cain Ballroom was Bob Wills and the Texas Playboys. From 1934 to 1945 they performed for dances about six days per week. These dances, hosted by Bob Wills and broadcast on KVOO Radio, were aired live Monday through Friday from 12:30 p.m. to 1:15 p.m. People listened faithfully to the forty-five minute radio show every day for several years. As Wills' popularity grew, so did that of the

Cain. During its busiest times in the 1940s, it was not uncommon to see several thousand people at or near the Cain Ballroom.

Eventually, time passed and the popularity of the big band era, including the dance halls such as the Cain Ballroom, began to decline. During the 1960s, the Cain was barely able to keep its doors open. It was a new generation, and in order to survive, the Cain had to adapt.

In order to make ends meet, the owners decided to start booking acts that the younger generation liked. This meant less dancing and more concerts. The decision to start booking rock groups revived the historic ballroom. The Cain was again sold in 1976 and several renovations were made to make it more suitable for concerts. Bands such as Van Halen, the Sex Pistols, Pat Benatar, the Police, Huey Lewis and the News, and others made appearances at the Cain Ballroom.

Of course, there are those who believe that the Cain Ballroom is haunted. Throughout its long history, some people apparently loved it so much that they decided to stay there after they died. To this day, there have been sightings of Bob Wills standing at the side of the main stage. He appears to be readying himself to go in front of the hundreds of people who packed the ballroom for his live radio broadcasts. This is rather an interesting haunting because most people who have claimed to have seen Bob Wills's ghost describe him as being younger, during the height of his popularity at the Cain Ballroom. In fact, Bob Wills died in 1975, several years after he stopped performing and doing radio shows at the Cain.

Another ghost at the Cain Ballroom has become known simply as Joan. Apparently, Joan is seen wearing a red dress that was popular in the late 1920s or early 1930s. That being the case, there is a possibility that she was a flapper. Some claim that she was an alcoholic who frequented the place when it was still known as the Louvre during Prohibition. Shortly before her apparition is experienced, the area tends to get several degrees colder.

Investigations of the Cain Ballroom have produced several EVPs of people laughing, various knocking sounds, and other miscellaneous noises that cannot readily be explained. According to one ghost hunter who investigated the Cain, there were several encounters with "shadow people" throughout the building. They also took several amazing photographs of misty forms in the areas reported to be haunted.

Brady Theater
105 W. Brady Street

Tate Brady was definitely one of the Tulsa's most influential men in the early part of the twentieth century. *The Encyclopedia of Oklahoma History and Culture* described Brady as a "pioneer, entrepreneur, member of the Oklahoma Bar, politician, and city booster of Tulsa." This would explain why several locations in Tulsa bear his name, including Brady Theater—which is located on West Brady Street. Not only was Brady personally responsible for bringing a considerable amount of business to Tulsa, he was also instrumental in creating two entertainment venues that still stand to this day—the Cain Ballroom and the Brady Theater.

Tate Brady broke ground for the theater in 1912, and work was not completed until two years later in 1914. Originally, the Brady Theater was known as the Tulsa Convention Center. This building was designed to be a place where large numbers of people could congregate for political and fraternal functions as well hosting some of the finest entertainment for miles around. The Brady was used as a vaudeville theater, and over the years the likes of Buddy Holly, Bill Cosby, Jerry Seinfeld, U2, and Green Day have all performed on its stage.

Although it has primarily been used for entertaining the masses, the Brady Theater has another, darker side associated with its history. Racial tensions had been running high for several years in Tulsa, Oklahoma, and on the evening of May 31, 1921, the tensions ignited into one of the deadliest days in Tulsa's history. Apparently, the Tulsa Race Riot started after a white female elevator worker claimed that a black man had assaulted her.

Word soon spread, and within hours several buildings in the Greenwood district were burned to the ground; masses were rioting; and people were dying. The reports of the fatalities vary considerably, from as few as 36 to as many as 300. By some accounts, up to 10,000 people were left homeless during the 16-hour riot.

According to most accounts, the Brady had been used as a detention center for black men during the Tulsa Race Riot. However, some believe that once the men were taken to the Brady Theater, they were severely beaten—in some cases, beaten to death. Although there is photographic evidence of people entering the Brady Theater during the Tulsa Race Riot of 1921, there appears to be no official documentation of what happened once the men were inside.

Ironically, 1921 appeared to be a very poignant year for the Brady Theater. This was the year that world-renowned opera tenor Enrico Caruso performed to a sold-out audience. According to local legend, Caruso wanted to be given a tour of Tulsa and the surrounding oil fields before his performance at the Brady Theater. He was in an open-air car, and it started to rain heavily and he was soaked. He returned to the Brady Theater just in time for the show. Accounts state that he developed pneumonia or bronchitis from the downpour and never fully recovered. He died a few months later in Naples, Italy, on August 2, 1921, at forty-eight years of age. Although some say that he died as a result of complications from his car ride in Tulsa, Oklahoma, it appears that he actually died from either pleurisy and empyema or peritonitis.

The Brady Theater is allegedly haunted by at least three different ghosts. The first ghost is that of Enrico Caruso himself. Although he actually died in Italy within a year after his performance in Tulsa, there are those who claim they have seen his ghost at the Brady Theater. Generally, he is seen close to the stage. He appears to be very solid only for a second, and has been known to disappear in front of astonished witnesses. In the area where Caruso's apparition has been seen is a cold spot that is frequently experienced. The sounds of footsteps have also been heard near the stage.

Another hotspot for paranormal activity is close to the men's bathroom in the Brady Theater. It is believed that this area is haunted by one or more of the black men who were allegedly killed while being detained at the theater during the Tulsa Race Riot. When a person goes into the bathroom where the beatings allegedly took place, there is an overwhelming sensation of pain and suffering. In addition, there have been sounds of men fighting, and the room stays ice cold even during the hottest of summer days.

A final ghost is likely that of a worker who fell off of his ladder and died at the Brady. It is uncertain whether he was one of the original builders of the Brady Theater or had been employed as a handyman after it was built. In regard to this ghost, employees have claimed to have found ladders moved from place to place throughout the theater.

Tulsa Garden Center
2435 S. Peoria Avenue

The Tulsa Garden Center was originally built as a private residence by David R. Travis, who had moved to Tulsa with his family from Ohio. Construction of the mansion started in 1919 and was completed two years later in 1921. The enormous mansion consisted of twenty-one separate rooms, including ten bathrooms. Some of the mansion's amenities included a lower-level ballroom, an arboretum, and a private library. There were several outbuildings constructed close to the mansion, including two greenhouses, two five-room cottages for guests, two barns, a swimming pool, and a solarium (or sunroom).

In 1923, J. Arthur Hull acquired the mansion from the brothers and decided to make several renovations, such as a sunken garden and conservatory for his wife Mary, shortly after moving into the mansion. Not long after J. Arthur Hull purchased the property, his wife Mary became pregnant. Sadly, Mary died in the home while giving birth to their baby. J. Arthur Hull made the necessary arrangements for Mary's body to lie in state in the alcove of the south sunroom so that her friends and family could pay their final respects before she was buried.

Eventually, Hull sold the mansion in 1934 and moved elsewhere. After switching hands a few times over the next twenty years, the property was sold to the City of Tulsa, which eventually transformed it to the Tulsa Garden Center.

It is uncertain as to how many distinct ghosts or spirits haunt the Tulsa Garden Center. Although some estimate there are as many as ten separate ghosts, it is more likely that three to five ghosts that haunt the garden center.

Not long after Mary's death, her apparition has been seen in both the sunroom and walking toward the library, which is in an entirely different part of the garned center. Sometimes, her apparition is accompanied by the sweet smell of fresh flowers.

Although Mary Hull is the only ghost that has been seen, other ghosts may be making their presence known in other ways, primarily through poltergeist activity. Over the years, caretakers have heard the sound of heavy footsteps pacing back and forth on the second floor. They have also noticed that the main door leading to the attic has been unlocked on several occasions, although they were alone at the time it occurred. Some suspect that these footsteps pacing back and forth could be associated with J. Arthur Hull himself.

Others have heard similar, heavy footsteps on the third-floor room that was once used as the servants' quarters. It is uncertain as to who may have been the source of these footsteps.

Other than the footsteps, there have been several electrical disturbances associated with the Tulsa Garden Center. Alarms have been triggered after the center was closed for the night, and upon investigation, there appeared to be no sign of break-in—there seemed to be no logical explanation why the alarms would be triggered at all. Along the same lines, employees and volunteers who have made certain that all of the lights were turned off before locking the garden center at night find that the library's lights are all turned on the next morning. It should be noted that although Mary Hull only lived in the house a short time before she died giving birth, she was known to frequent the library. Similarly, employees have found all of the French doors on the first floor to be wide open when they arrive in the morning.

Pawhuska

Constantine Theater
110 W Main Street

Originally, the building that would become known as the Constantine Theater was a local hotel simply named the Pawhuska Hotel. Its main clientele consisted of traveling salesmen and Native Americans from the Osage tribe who came to Pawhuska to conduct business.

A man by the name of C. A. Constantine purchased the hotel in 1914 and decided to convert it into a theater for the residents of Pawhuska and rename it the Constantine Theater. For thirteen years, the Constantine Theater had live theater and vaudeville acts from around the country. In 1927, Constantine sold the theater, which was converted from a live theater to a movie theater. Because of the name recognition, the new owner decided to keep the name Constantine Theater when he reopened it. It remained open as a movie theater until the 1960s, when it closed and became abandoned.

In regard to ghosts that have been associated with the Constantine, two separate hauntings have been consistently reported over the years. Most often, people who have paranormal experiences at this theater claim to hear footsteps going across the stage. Because of the light sound of the footsteps, it is believed to be the sound of a woman wearing heels as opposed to somebody wearing heavier shoes or boots. Sometimes these footsteps are preceded by the sound of a man and woman arguing. Most paranormal investigators believe that these are the ghosts of Constantine having an argument with his daughter, Sappho. An apparition that has been seen throughout the first floor has been identified to be that of C. A. Constantine himself.

Another ghost that can be traced back to the days of the Pawhuska Hotel is that of Ada Frye, a twenty-year-old woman who died at the hotel of typhoid fever in 1906. As she was new to the area and had few contacts, the hotel manager thought it right to give her a proper burial, including making certain that she was buried in a white dress. They did so, right at the hotel, and arranged for her to be buried in a nearby cemetery. There are those who claim that they have seen a young woman wearing a white dress near the hotel room where she died.

Guthrie

....

Ella Myers

Near the Santa Fe Right of Way

Perhaps one of the most intriguing ghost stories ever documented in Guthrie, Oklahoma, concerns a woman by the name of Ella (aka Lula) Myers, who was found dead in the home of Ella Horton in the spring of 1896. Over several days, the *Guthrie Daily Leader* had several articles about the mysterious death and subsequent haunting by Ella Myers.

On Sunday, April 5, 1896, the body of Ella Myers, a prostitute, was found unconscious or dead in the home of Ella Horton. It is believed that Ella Horton was a prostitute herself or a madame who oversaw several local ladies of the night. Although the street address was not given in any of the newspaper articles, they did report that the house in which she died was "near the Santa Fe right of way."

After Ella Myers's body was hastily examined by the Guthrie coroner and a physician by the name of Dr. Cotteral, it was ordered to be buried immediately. According to the coroner, the official cause of death was overdose by cocaine, as Myers was known to be addicted to the substance, which was legal at that time. However, there was no independent way to confirm or deny the cause of death because of what happened next.

As Myers had no money, she was buried in a hastily constructed pine coffin within a few hours of being seen by the coroner and Dr. Cottreal. Her body was buried in a pauper's grave in a nearby graveyard early the next day. There were several rumors associated with the hasty burial of Myers's body. One was that the coroner and/or Dr. Cottreal had been one of Ella's clients and they wanted to be rid of her body as soon as possible. Other rumors even went as far as to allege that she in fact was alive when she was seen by the men, who had arranged to have her buried alive, face down in the coffin. There was a great deal of controversy regarding the condition of Myers's body. Although the coroner and his associate claimed that Ella Myers's body was freshly dead, the undertaker, Dr. Baker, stated that she had been dead for quite some time and that her body was "badly decomposed."

According to the four newspaper articles from the *Guthrie Daily Leader* dated April 9 to April 23, 1896, the paranormal activity began soon after Ella Myers was buried.

Shortly after Myers was buried, people who walked by the shack where she was found would hear loud moans of despair as well as deep, heartwrenching sobbing. Also, although the shack was no longer occupied and had been locked from the outside, the sounds of voices came from inside. When people went to investigate the sounds and opened the door to enter, it would slam in their face although there did not appear to be anybody inside the house .

Soon, things really began to get interesting at the house where Ella Myers was found dead or near death. In the April 15, 1896, edition of the *Guthrie Daily Leader*, a local resident described as a "well-known sport" decided to see if there was any truth in what was being written about Ella Myers in the newspaper. In a later edition of the paper, the man was identified as local socialite George Hardies.

Skeptical of the newspaper reports and what he had been hearing from other people, Hardies went to investigate the house himself because he just could not believe what had been written about the ghost of Ella Myers.

Just as with the other accounts, Hardies attempted to open the door, but it would not open for him. After trying for a few moments, it opened easily and he entered. As soon as he entered the room, he claimed that he saw a blood-red hand carrying a vial or glass. Hardies did not stay around very long to get a closer look. As soon as he left the house, he apparently went to the local newspaper to tell his story. After the story was published on April 15, 1898, it piqued the interests of several spiritualists in the area. Within a day or two of the April 15 article, as many as twenty-five spiritualists and psychics decided to visit the house to see if they could make contact with the ghost of Ella Myers.

Virtually everyone who went there heard the moaning and crying from within the locked shack. Some peeked in the window and saw a woman in white standing by herself. At least two people who congregated there identified her as Ella or Lula Myers.

However, perhaps the most interesting and possibly incriminating experience from the whole incident was that some people allegedly heard the ghost of Lula Myers. On three separate occasions, people present at the house distinctly heard a woman's voice cry out. "Don't give me any more morphine. I am sick." It was commonly known that Myers was addicted to cocaine, not morphine. There were those who believed that Ella Myers was given a large amount of morphine shortly before her death either to prevent an overdose ... or to prevent her from talking. The woman's plea gave credence in some circles that the doctor who examined her body actually gave her a shot of morphine in order to kill her. However, to this day that allegation has not been substantiated.

From the time of her death on April 9, 1896, until April 22, 1896, the ghost of Ella Myers caused quite a commotion for people who lived near the house where she died. Sounds of crying and moaning could be heard constantly from the house. People were at the house at all hours trying to get a peek at her specter. Some residents were so frustrated by the new-found fame of their recently deceased neighbor that they temporarily left their homes. The newspaper article from the April 19, 1896, edition went as far as to write "for over a week, supernatural manifestations in the house have aroused the neighborhood, and the shacks in the vicinity of the haunted dwelling have been vacated."

The wailing, crying, apparitions, and other manifestations continued to make news until April 22, 1896, when Ella's brother arrived from Kansas to claim her body. According to the last newspaper article, dated April 23, 1896, word of Ella Myers's death had reached her brother. After reading the first three articles, her brother came to Guthrie and claimed her body and returned it to Kansas, where it was given a proper burial. Authorities who were there during the exhumation confirmed that Ella's body was buried face-up and there was no indication (such as scratch marks on the inside of the coffin) that she was buried alive. Ironically, after her body was taken back to Kansas by her brother, there were apparently no more signs of paranormal activity.

Guthrie First Territorial Prison
Second and Noble

Fifteen years before Oklahoma became a state in 1907, the First Territorial Prison in Guthrie was constructed of brick and dark limestone taken from a local quarry. Because of the dark color of the limestone used in the Guthrie Territorial Prison, locals and prisoners alike gave it the nickname of the "Black Jail."

Rumor had it that the Territorial Prison was escape-proof because the limestone walls were an average of eighteen inches thick. In addition, the lower level was actually underground and under close guard much of the time, which made any attempts of escape next to impossible. The construction of the Black Jail and its claim to be escape-proof was also likely its undoing. The dark limestone and brick walls offered no insulation from the Oklahoma weather. The winters were cold and damp and as a result, many of the inmates were in poor health much of the winter. In the summer, the inside of the jail was sweltering because there was no ventilation to speak of. In essence, the summer days made the prison into a veritable oven, and many inmates suffered from dehydration and in some cases heat exhaustion.

Close to the time Oklahoma became a state, the prison was closed down and the inmates were transferred to other federal institutions to finish out their sentences. For a period of time, the Black Jail was vacant.

Seeing that the jail was for sale and was a relatively sound structure, the Nazarene Church purchased it. The building that had once been one of the most feared federal prisons in this part of the country had been converted into a Church of the Nazarene. After many renovations were made, the building soon became one of the area's most prosperous churches and had congregation members from Guthrie and surrounding communities. The Black Jail was used as a Nazarene Church until the early 1970s, when the church decided to move to another location. For several years, the Guthrie Territorial Prison remained unoccupied.

Eventually, the former prison was purchased by a group known as the Samaritan Foundation, who turned the building into a makeshift orphanage for young children. The Samaritan Foundation used the prison for several years until, in the 1990s, the local Department of Health and Human Resources was called over concern about the living conditions of the children. An investigation from the DHHR determined that, although the building had been renovated by both the Nazarene Church and the Samaritan Foundation, the living conditions were simply not adequate for the children, primarily due to the lack of ventilation and insulation. As a result, the Samaritan Foundation decided to move their facility elsewhere in the mid-1990s and once again the prison was abandoned.

With being a prison, a church, and an orphanage, there was ample opportunity for the Black Jail of Guthrie, Oklahoma, to have its share of ghosts.

The most prominent ghost associated with the Black Jail is that of James Phillips, prisoner of the Territorial Prison until his unexpected death in 1907.

James Phillips was convicted of murdering a Guthrie, Oklahoma, resident and was sentenced to die by hanging. Until the hanging was to take place, Phillips was held in solitary confinement in the prison's basement level. As there had been no hangings in the Guthrie area for quite some time, finding a location for the execution was a bit of a problem. So, it was decided that a scaffold be built specifically for the hanging of Phillips. However, it just so happened that the scaffold was built on Noble Street directly across from the Black Jail in direct view of Phillips's cell.

The problem with this location was that each day that passed allowed Phillips to see the gallows where he would be hanged come closer and closer to completion. Watching its construction must have been very traumatizing for James Phillips.

Not long before Phillips was to hang, he was found dead in his cell by prison guards. The cause of death was determined to be heart failure as a result of being forced to watch his own scaffold and gallows literally being built in front of him. In essence, the poor man died of fright.

The emotional turmoil that James Phillips experienced shortly before his death must have left a form of psychic impression on his cell and the surrounding area. Shortly after his death, guards and other visitors throughout the years have claimed to have heard footsteps from within the cell and all along the hallway near the cell. In addition, there have been several accounts of a man looking out of one of the basement windows toward Noble Street. The window that the apparition can be seen is none other than James Phillips's old cell. People who were close enough to see the face in detail say that it had the expression of intense fear or horror on it. Finally, there have been accounts of the sounds of a man crying heard from Phillips's cell.

Other incidents throughout the building that have been attributed to its days as a federal prison. The sound of men's voices have been heard on the first floor and on the basement level in the hallways. The sound of steel doors being slammed have been recorded by amateur ghost hunters, even though all but one of the steel doors have been removed. People who have visited the prison have also claimed to have seen brief apparitions of the prisoners out of the corner of their eye in several of the cells. There is even one cell where the sound of a man coughing can be heard.

Another ghost associated with the Black Jail comes from its days as a Nazarene Church. On the ground floor near the main entrance, the sound of a woman singing can be heard on occasion, although the area is usually vacant at the time. Several people have also seen the apparition of a woman wearing a long dress cross Noble Street and walk toward the main entrance of the prison. Generally, the apparition is seen later in the afternoon or early evening. It is possible that both of these ghosts are actually of the same person who was likely a member of the congregation of the Nazarene Church.

Finally, the sounds of children playing and laughing have been heard by people who have visited the prison. These sounds are not typically found inside the building, but rather outside. These are possibly the ghosts of children who were either members of the Nazarene Church or more likely the voices of some of the children who stayed at the prison while it was owned by the Samaritan Foundation.

Arapaho

Arapaho Cemetery

Outside of the small town of Arapaho, Oklahoma, is a dusty road that leads to a small, nondescript cemetery. In that cemetery is the tombstone of Robina Smith. She died unexpectdly in a tragic automobile accident on Highway 183 in 1936, when she was only nineteen years old. Although she died violently and unexpectedly, this ghost story is not about Robina at all. It concerns her father, George Smith.

George Smith was a very decent, God-fearing man who had wanted more than anything for his daughter and other loved ones to be saved by Jesus Christ. George asked his daughter to turn her life over to God on several occasions, but she did not do so before she died. Perhaps she thought that she could do it at some point in the future.

In any case, George was grief stricken not only by his daughter's death, but by the fact that she died unsaved and a sinner. He never quite got over her death and grieved over her until his own death in 1972.

After George Smith's death, visitors to the cemetery who have walked near Robina's gravesite can sometimes hear the sound of a man sobbing uncontrollably and crying out loud, "Oh no! Oh, my God! Robina has not been saved!" Those who have heard this voice have included a church pastor who had visited the cemetery after a graveside service. Another witness was one of George's old friends, who recognized the disembodied voice as that of George lamenting over his daughter's death.

FIVE

TEXAS

186 miles

Although Route 66 spans nearly 200 miles of the northern panhandle of Texas, there were only about twenty towns located directly along the route. But after Route 66 was decommissioned, the effect on most of these towns was nothing short of catastrophic.

In Texas, there are an estimated 700 ghost towns, shells of once-prosperous towns of days gone by. Several of the towns that were found along Route 66 are not even on today's roadmaps. Some of these ghost towns offer little more than abandoned gas stations, businesses, and homes to let us know that they even existed at all. As each year passes, the number of people who remember these towns firsthand decreases, and

Wichita Falls

soon we will have to rely on photographs and written accounts to let us know what these towns were like when they were more prosperous.

While doing research for this chapter, I was only able to find a handful of stories from Texas towns that were along Route 66. Many of the towns that were along the Mother Road in Texas simply no longer exist. With that in mind, I decided to expand the listing of ghost stories in this chapter to include locations that are a few hours' drive from Route 66. This will give you an opportunity to read about some of the wonderful locations and ghost stories that the Lone Star State has to offer.

Denton

Old Alton Bridge/Argyle Bridge
Copper Canyon Road

The Old Alton, aka the Argyle Bridge, was built in 1884 over a shallow area of Hickory Creek that cowboys once used to cross while moving their herds of cattle cross-country. Argyle Bridge was constructed to make it easier to travel between the towns of Copper Canyon and Devon, Texas. It was named the Old Alton Bridge because of its proximity to the small town of Alton, which no longer exists. Argyle Bridge was open for vehicle traffic until 2001, when a new bridge for cars and trucks was built a short distance away. The bridge is still open for pedestrians and bicyclists to safely cross Hickory Creek.

Although known as either the Argyle or Old Alton Bridge, most locals refer to it as the Goatman's Bridge. According to local legend, a horned man-goat can sometimes be seen near the bridge, especially just before a disaster is reported. The goat-man allegedly lives in the woods nearby and is always waiting to pounce upon unsuspecting people who cross his bridge. It is unlikely that this type of creature ever existed in real life, but legends such as this can have some minute basis in fact.

The truth is that there really was a goat-man associated with the Old Alton Bridge. In the early 1900s, an African-American farmer by the name of Oscar Washburn lived on a farm close to Alton. Washburn was known as a very honest man. He made his living by raising and selling livestock, especially goats, to local farmers and butchers.

Because of the reasonable prices and excellent quality of his livestock, people started to travel from other towns to buy their goats from Washburn. As his business increased, Washburn decided to make it easier for new customers to find his farm. On the far side of the Old Alton Bridge, Washburn erected a hand-painted sign with the words "This Way to the Goat Man's" written in large, bold letters.

Unfortunately, the first part of the twentieth century was a time of racial tension in Texas and throughout the United States. A group of local businessmen who may have had connections to the Ku Klux Klan were not impressed with Washburn's success. They felt that his increased business was costing them money.

Late one night in August 1938, a group of hooded men, including several of these businessmen, kidnapped Washburn from his home and took him to the Old Alton Bridge with the intention of hanging him over the edge until he was dead. Washburn's hands were bound behind his back and, although he struggled, the men succeeded in placing a noose around his neck and threw him off the Old Alton Bridge.

The men waited for a few minutes and looked over the side of the bridge to make certain that Washburn was dead. To their surprise, when they pulled up the rope, they realized that Washburn had somehow escaped. Infuriated, the men scoured the area for Washburn, but could only find some footprints on the far side of the creek where he had climbed out of the water. The footprints were going in the direction of Washburn's farm, so the men decided to pay his farm another visit.

In retaliation, this group of men returned to Washburn's farm and murdered his wife and two small children. While Washburn likely attempted to go home to warn his family, he was unable to reach them in time. After that night, Oscar Washburn was never seen or heard from again. His livestock were released and left to wander the wilderness. Soon after, the legend of the goat-man of the Old Alton Bridge was born.

There are some ghosts associated with the Old Alton Bridge and surrounding area. On certain nights, people who go near the bridge have claimed to have seen a large number of floating lights together on the bridge. Sometimes, these lights are accompanied by a number of misty or shadowy forms grouped together. The shadowy forms could very well be the ghosts of the businessmen who abducted Washburn and killed his family. The lights could simply be the apparition of the torches that they were carrying with them that night.

There are other reported hauntings associated with the Old Alton Bridge itself. There have been reports that the sounds of splashes of what can be described as a man frantically running or struggling can be heard in the creek below. Another ghost that is associated with the bridge may very well be Washburn himself. Sometimes, an African-American man can be seen crossing the bridge with a large herd of goats. This apparition will generally disappear about halfway across the bridge, which is where the businessmen attempted to hang Washburn.

The bridge itself is not the only haunting associated with the events of that night in 1938. Today, very few people know where Washburn's home stands. However, the few people who know its location also believe that it is haunted. They have reported hearing the sounds of a woman and young children crying.

Mineral Wells

Baker Hotel
200 East Hubbard Street
The Baker Hotel was a fourteen-story, 452-room hotel built in Mineral Wells, Texas, by entrepreneur and millionaire T. B. Baker at an estimated cost of $1,250,000. In the 1920s, this was a considerable investment, but Baker felt that opening the hotel was worth the risk. The Baker Hotel

opened its doors to the public on November 9, 1929. It was by far the tallest building in Mineral Wells at this time and was nicknamed the Grand Old Lady because of its size and its architectural beauty.

Baker invested so much money into this project because of the natural mineral springs surrounding Mineral Wells. According to Baker and residents of Mineral Wells, the area's mineral springs had healing properties that could cure anything from stomachaches to wrinkles to certain mental illnesses. Baker thought that people would come from all over the country and pay for the opportunity to soak in these waters.

Baker spared no expense in making the Baker Hotel as luxurious as possible for his guests. In addition to the 452 rooms, the Baker Hotel had two complete spas that used only the local mineral water, two Olympic-sized swimming pools, a state-of-the art indoor gymnasium, several meeting rooms, and two large ballrooms found on the first floor (the Brazos Room) and fourteenth floor (the Sky Room) of the hotel.

For several years after the Baker Hotel opened, it was the place to be noticed for the nation's rich and famous. People flocked to consume and to soak in the mineral waters, claiming that the water really did have healing properties. Some of the biggest names in Hollywood were known to frequent the hotel. It has been said that Clark Gable, Judy Garland, Will Rogers, Lawrence Welk, and other famous celebrities and millionaires considered the Baker Hotel one of their favorite retreats.

One of the most interesting features of the Baker Hotel was that it contained three separate sets of staircases for its guests. The most pronounced and elaborate was the main staircase that led directly to the main hotel lobby. This was primarily for the rich and famous people who wanted to be noticed when they made an entrance.

The second staircase was dedicated to the hotel staff. Rather than having the staff interacting with the guests, a separate staircase was built so that they could do their work in the different rooms without interruption. This proved to be very efficient, especially to the several maids who had a full job of making certain that the hotel's rooms were cleaned each day. It also prevented the staff from having the opportunity to bother the celebrities for autographs.

The third staircase was designed to cater to those hotel guests who wished to make a more discreet entrance or exit. This staircase was out of view from the main lobby so people could get to their rooms in relative privacy. This was especially useful for the hotel guest planning a secret rendezvous with a mistress or anyone interested in going to a room where alcohol was served during Prohibition, which was in place until 1933. Also, as many celebrities of the day were guests at the Baker Hotel, they often used it to go to their room without being bothered.

The Baker Hotel was very popular among the wealthy and famous well into the late 1950s. By this time, the fad of the mineral waters had faded somewhat, and eventually the number of people who came to the Baker Hotel started to decrease. The hotel was so large, and guests were not as frequent as in the 1930s and 1940s, that upkeep simply cost more than the hotel was bringing in with revenue. As a result, the Baker Hotel closed its doors for the first time in 1963.

Rather than watch the hotel remain empty, private investors banded together and arranged for the hotel to reopen in 1965. This renaissance of the Baker Hotel did not last long, and it once again closed in 1973 due to the extreme cost of running the hotel. After it closed in 1973, the hotel never reopened for business, although for a few years in the 1980s people were able to tour several sections of the Baker Hotel. Eventually, these tours ended, and the Baker Hotel has been vacant ever since.

There have been reports of paranormal activity at the Baker Hotel since the early 1950s. Based on the number of separate ghosts known to haunt the Baker Hotel, it has earned the reputation as one of the most haunted places in this part of Texas. Several parts of this hotel have been hotspots for ghostly sightings since the 1950s.

Most of the ghosts associated with the Baker Hotel were of people who came to the Mineral Wells area and to the hotel to benefit from the healing properties of the mineral waters. Desperately looking for a cure for their respective ailments, people would often forgo traditional medicinal.

Granted, the mineral waters may have been beneficial for some ailments, but this was not the case for everybody. Some people with terminal diseases such as advanced cancer would make the trip to the Baker Hotel only to find that they were too weak to leave. It was not uncommon for hotel staff to find that one of their hotel guests had died while staying at the Baker Hotel. Perhaps this is why there are so many ghosts associated with the Baker Hotel.

The main lobby of the Baker Hotel has at least two separate ghosts that have made their presence known since even before it closed for the first time in 1963. The first ghost is that of a young boy who had been confined to a wheelchair. He was likely ill when his parents or other caretakers brought him to the Baker Hotel in hopes that the mineral water would cure whatever disease had confined him to the wheelchair. It is likely that he died in Mineral Wells, and likely at the Baker Hotel itself. This boy has been seen in his wheelchair at the bottom of the main staircase. He has also been seen looking out of one of the windows on the first floor of the hotel.

The second ghost that is associated with the Baker Hotel's lobby is heard rather than seen. On several occasions, there has been the distinct sound of a woman wearing high heels walking across the lobby floor. The sound has been so loud on occasion as to actually echo across the large, empty hotel lobby.

The Brazos Room on the first floor was one of the Baker Hotel's two main ballrooms. This room is another part of the hotel where a considerable amount of paranormal activity can be experienced. There have been instances in which big band music and the sound of loud chatter and people in conversation can be heard—as if there was a large party in the room. It is of note that some big band celebrities of the day were known to put on concerts in this room. The Brazos Room was often used to host elaborate parties, so that could be a likely explanation for these sounds. In addition to the apparitions and the disembodied sounds of music and voices, several orbs have been photographed on numerous occasions, and the scent of freshly cooked food is reported to be wafting throughout the room. Also, electronic devices such as cameras also tend to malfunction or have their batteries drained while in the Brazos Room, which is another possible sign of paranormal activity.

Although most of the ghosts associated with the Baker Hotel are associated with sick people who were looking for a remedy to their illness, there are other reasons the hotel may be haunted. According to several sources, the hotel kitchen was the site of a murder. Local legend has it that a married male cook was having an affair with a maid. One night in the kitchen, the two got into an argument and the mistress threatened to tell the cook's wife about their affair. He became infuriated and in the heat of their fight stabbed her to death in the kitchen. After the murder, people have heard a woman screaming and crying in the area she was killed. There have also been photographs of misty forms that have been taken in the kitchen by ghost hunters who were fortunate enough to investigate the Baker Hotel.

The Mezzanine Floor above the main lobby sometimes has the strong smell of cigar smoke, although nobody is smoking at the time. This is one of the oldest-reported paranormal activities at the Baker Hotel, as there have been reports of the cigar smell since the mid-1950s.

The seventh floor has a room that is likely one of the most haunted areas of the entire hotel. This ghost is of a woman who allegedly committed suicide by jumping from the window of her hotel room, which was located in the northeast corner of the seventh floor. According to most accounts, the woman was named Virginia and described as a beautiful redhead in her mid-twenties. Virginia was the mistress to Mr. T. B. Baker, the hotelier himself. Before the hotel was closed for the last time in 1973, maids would find the door ajar and the window open. On one occasion, a maid found a water glass with lip prints on it and the window open. Even after the hotel closed permanently, people walking on the sidewalk outside of the Baker Hotel would sometimes see Virginia looking out of her window on the seventh floor.

Another haunted area of the Baker Hotel is the Baker Suite on the tenth floor. This is the suite T. B. Baker stayed at frequently right after the hotel opened in 1929 and returned to shortly before his death in 1972, just one year before the hotel closed permanently. There have been several sightings of a ghost fitting Baker's description standing in the Baker Suite. He has also been seen pacing the hallway outside of the suite and, on more than one occasion, outside the room of his mistress, Virginia, which was located on the seventh floor. People who have stayed in the Baker Suite on the tenth floor who did not witness Baker's apparition have commented on the strong feeling of being watched.

Waxahachie

Catfish Plantation
814 Water Street

The Catfish Plantation is a three-story Victorian house on Water Street in Waxahachie, Texas. Built in 1895, it served as a private residence until the 1970s. The house was purchased in the mid-1980s and converted into a restaurant specializing in fine Southern and Cajun cuisine. In addition to the down-home atmosphere and wonderful food, the Catfish Plantation is also reportedly haunted by no fewer than three former residents who died in the house years before it became a restaurant.

The oldest haunting associated with the restaurant is that of a young woman by the name of Elizabeth Anderson, the daughter of the farmer who built the house in 1895. The story goes that on Elizabeth's wedding day, a jealous ex-boyfriend entered the house and murdered her while she was still wearing her white wedding dress. Elizabeth was about twenty years old, and according to one website had "brown eyes, straight, fine, light brown hair, which she wore close to her head." Over the years, those who have seen Elizabeth's ghost in the dining room or looking out the bay window have all offered a similar description.

Elizabeth's ghost is usually confined to two parts of the house—she is seen in the dining room and looking out a bay window in the front room where she was killed. Elizabeth's apparition has often been accompanied by the sweet smell of roses, which were reportedly her favorite flower and might have been the flowers in her wedding bouquet. On one occasion, a séance was conducted in the dining room and much to everybody's surprise a full specter of Elizabeth manifested itself and was again accompanied by the smell of roses.

A second ghost at the Catfish Plantation is that of Bill "Will" Buyers, a farmer who died of pneumonia during the Great Depression. Will's ghost can be seen mostly on the front porch. He is described as a man wearing bib overalls. The Catfish Plantation literature describes Will as a friendly spirit who often flirts with female guests by running his fingers through their hair or putting his ghostly hand upon their knees.

The third ghost is that of a Caroline Jenkins Mooney, a woman who lived in the house with her husband from 1953 until she died of health problems associated with old age in 1970. Her ghost is mostly experienced in the restaurant's kitchen. Unlike the ghosts of Elizabeth or Will, Caroline often makes herself known through poltergeist activity, particularly in the kitchen. It is believed that Caroline still considers the home to be hers and is trying to scare people away from "her" kitchen. On occasion, the lights in the kitchen and dining room have been known to turn themselves off although nobody is nowhere near a light switch. Other times, dinnerware, food, and utensils have been flung at restaurant employees working in the kitchen.

In addition to the three identified ghosts, other miscellaneous paranormal events have taken place at the restaurant. Bluish orbs have been seen with the naked eye in several of the vacant rooms. Many of these orbs have been photographed and recorded on film. Other times, in the many cold spots that appear randomly, electronic equipment will malfunction and lose all power. This is particularly frustrating to the paranormal investigators who have investigated the Catfish Plantation over the years. Because of all the paranormal activity, the Catfish Plantation, has been the focus of several newspaper and magazine articles and been featured on the Discovery Channel's *Ghost Lab* in November 2009.

Becky Road

About six miles north of the Catfish Plantation is Becky Road, which was where the last Confederate soldier of the Civil War was reportedly hanged. His name was Private John Hemerich, and he was captured by a group of Union soldiers and taken to a remote section of Becky Road. At the roadside, Hemerich was hanged from a tree. In the years since Hemerich's execution, people who have traveled down Becky Road have seen a young man about twenty years old standing at the side of the road wearing a Confederate uniform. Others have even claimed to have seen a phantom soldier hanging from a tree along the same stretch of road.

Jacksboro

Fort Richardson

Highway 281 S

During the early to mid-nineteenth century, this area of Texas was a very rugged and difficult place for settlers to live. In addition to diseases and food shortages that all settlers typically faced, there was the added threat of attacks for indigenous tribes such as the Apache and Comanche who considered the settlers to be a threat. In order to assist with the taming of the West, a series of forts were constructed to protect the settlers. Fort Richardson was one of these forts.

Constructed in 1867, Fort Richardson was named after a Union general by the name of Israel B. Richardson, who was fatally wounded in the Battle of Antietam. As a memorial to his heroism and sacrifice, the fort was named after him.

The fort was instrumental in helping the settlers thrive, but after eleven years, Jacksboro was starting to thrive and there had not been a single attack on the settlers' families by the Apache and Comanche in quite some time. In May of 1878, Fort Richardson was decommissioned and the soldiers stationed there were transferred.

For several years after it was decommissioned, Fort Richardson remained abandoned. Several of the fort's buildings were destroyed by constant exposure to the elements. In 1963, the Texas State Parks and Wildlife Department recognized the historical significance of Fort Richardson and within a few years, reconstruction commenced and there was an attempt to save as many of the fort's original structures as possible. The buildings that could not be saved were carefully reconstructed to closely resemble the original buildings. In 1973, Fort Richardson State Park officially opened and has been in operation since.

Only seven of the original buildings at Fort Richardson could be saved: the morgue, hospital, officers' quarters, commissary, guardhouse, powder magazine, and bakery. Most of the hauntings at Fort Richardson are said to take place in three of these original buildings.

The Fort Richardson hospital is considered by most ghost hunters to be the fort's most haunted building. There have been sightings of Union soldiers pacing back and forth on the porch and in front of the hospital windows after the fort is closed. The loud sound of footsteps can also be heard on the hospital porch. Some people who have heard these footsteps claim that the sound will sometimes follow them throughout the hospital until they leave the building.

Not far from the hospital is the fort's morgue. Life on the frontier was harsh, and it was not uncommon to have settlers or soldiers die from natural threats in the area, attacks from hostiles, or after being admitted to the fort hospital. The bodies of those who died were taken to the morgue until burial arrangements were made. The ghost of a Union soldier has been seen standing at attention in front of the morgue's main entryway. Sometimes the soldier appears so solid that he has been mistaken for a Civil War reenactor. At other times, the soldier's apparition is somewhat more misty and tends to disappear entirely just above his knees.

The third building at Fort Richardson that is haunted is the officers' quarters. As with the hospital and morgue, the officers' quarters is haunted by several ghosts that appear to be wearing Union uniforms. Sometimes these ghosts are simply standing beside the doorway or looking out the window, while at other times they appear to be interacting with one another. In addition to the apparitions of the Union soldiers, lights that may be from lanterns or candles can be seen inside of the windows of the officers' quarters late at night. People who attempt to investigate the s lights are unable to find a physical source of origin.

Granbury

Granbury Opera House
116 S. Houston Street

One of the legends associated with the Granbury Opera House concerns a mysterious man by the name of John St. Helen. If the story surrounding John St. Helen has any truth to it, this man was known by another, more infamous name ... John Wilkes Booth, the man who assassinated Abraham Lincoln on April 14, 1865 at Ford's Theater in Washington, D.C.

Most people believe that Booth did die in a barn fire at Richard Garrett's farm twelve days after assassinating Abraham Lincoln. However, some people believe that Booth did not die that night and in fact escaped. They believe that the man who died at the Garrett farm was actually named James William Boyd, a Confederate officer who held an uncanny physical resemblance to Booth. Boyd was captured by Union troops in 1863 and was a prisoner of war until 1865, when he was granted his release to take care of his seven children after their mother died. Boyd made plans to meet his son in Brownsville, Texas. However, Boyd did not show up to meet his son and was never heard from again. Those who follow this theory claim that it was Boyd's body that had been burned in the fire at Garrett's farm so that the investigators chasing Booth did not have to admit that he had escaped. Once Boyd was dead, his body was adulterated to resemble Booth, including the breaking of his left leg and adding a telltale tattoo with the initials JWB on his left hand that Booth was known to have.

There does appear to be some anecdotal evidence indicating that Booth did not die on April 26, 1865, at Richard Garrett's farm. According to the 1907 book *Escape and Suicide of John Wilkes Booth*, author Finis L. Bates wrote that Booth left the Washington, D.C., area and settled in Granbury, Texas, using the pseudonym of John St. Helen.

John St. Helen appeared in Granbury, Texas, a few months after Lincoln's assassination. He claimed to be a teacher from the eastern United States, but rarely talked about his past. When asked why he moved to Texas, he would just say that he had always wanted to move out West.

John St. Helen shared several physical and personality traits with John Wilkes Booth. Both had a liking for alcohol and were known to be intoxicated in public on occasion. John St. Helen had a distinct limp with his left leg—the leg that Booth broke when he jumped from the balcony after shooting Lincoln. Like Booth, John St. Helen would quote Shakespeare during everyday conversation.

Despite his alcoholism, St. Helen became well-known and liked in Granbury. He was even invited to the wedding of the daughter of wealthy local businessman. The reception took place the night before the wedding and St. Helen and many of the other more affluent people from Granbury were in attendance.

One of the people at the event was an agent from Washington, D.C., who had been investigating the assassination of Lincoln and had doubts about the official story concerning Booth's death in the fire on Garrett's farm. This agent took St. Helen aside and claimed that he knew his true identity. According to the story, John St. Helen did not deny these allegations outright, but claimed to have proof that he was not John Wilkes Booth. John St. Helen told the agent that he would be happy to sit with him the following day to answer any questions because he did not want to make a scene at the wedding reception. Surprisingly, the agent agreed to this, possibly out of respect for the soon-to-be bride's father. St. Helen excused himself from the party and left into the night, never to be seen by the agent or residents of Granbury, Texas, again.

After leaving Granbury, John St. Helen settled into another part of Texas, where he changed his name again. In the late 1870s or early 1880s, John St. Helen became quite ill and sought medical attention from the town doctor. St. Helen felt that he was near death and decided to share his story with the doctor, including the fact that he was John Wilkes Booth.

Upon hearing this, the doctor excused himself, promising that he would return soon to check on his condition. John St. Helen grew suspicious when the doctor was gone an excessive amount of time. When the doctor did return to "John St. Helen's" bed with authorities, they found that the bed was empty. After this, very little is known about the fate of this man. Most believe that shortly after he left the doctor's care, he died. Others believe that he lived a few years longer before killing himself while intoxicated. No matter what the final fate of John St. Helen, the question of whether he was indeed John Wilkes Booth remains unanswered.

Why is this story included in a book of ghost stories along Route 66? There is a paranormal twist to John St. Helen's life that takes place at the Granbury Opera House. When he was not getting drunk or teaching, John St. Helen frequented the Granbury Opera House and even helped with the performances. On several occasions, John St. Helen even acted in plays that were performed at the theater.

After John St. Helen left Granbury so abruptly, there have been several sightings of a man fitting St. Helen's description limping on stage just before and after a performance. Sometimes this apparition is accompanied by the strong smell of liquor. On at least one occasion, ghost hunters investigating the Granbury Opera House have claimed to have recorded EVPs of a male voice quoting a few lines from Shakespeare.

Arlington

River Legacy Park
701 West Green Oaks Boulevard

There is a local legend in Arlington that River Legacy Park was once used in the Civil War by a group of Confederate soldiers to take captured Union troops. Apparently, in a secluded area of the park there is an old, rusty gate, the original purpose of which has been long forgotten.

The story goes that when Union soldiers were captured, most were brought to the area and hanged from one of the many trees surrounding the gate. Some were tied and forced to their knees before being shot execution style. After they were killed, the bodies would be taken to an undisclosed location nearby and buried in shallow graves. As the gate was one of the last things that the Union soldiers saw before they were killed, it soon became known as Hell's Gate.

The man responsible for ordering most of the executions was a Confederate general of Irish descent. It has been estimated that this man either personally executed or oversaw the executions of nearly one hundred Union soldiers unlucky enough to cross his path.

Today, there have been stories told that the sounds of men sobbing and pleading can be heard followed by the sound of gunfire. The red-haired Confederate general has also been seen either walking with sword drawn or on horseback near Hell's Gate.

Railroad Crossing

The railroad crossing one mile west of Arlington was the scene of a deadly automobile accident on October 7, 1912. According to newspaper reports, six people, ranging in age from six to thirty-six years, were hit by a train while in a vehicle driving home from Arlington. The force of the impact split the car entirely in two and caused body parts and debris to be spread up to two hundred yards from the scene of the accident.

People who have been near the scene of the accident years afterward have seen a man walking with his head bowed and his hands in his pockets. Some believe that he is the ghost of Rufus Cornelius, the thirty-six-year-old driver of the vehicle and may be looking for his other family members. There have also been accounts from people who have heard the sound of metal against metal as the train hits the vehicle.

Wichita Falls

Holiday Creek Reservoir

A young man by the name of Tom apparently met his end after a night of partying at the Holiday Creek Reservoir. There are several versions of this tale, but in most Tom was a local college student who had a bit too much to drink one night. As he was walking along the Holiday Creek Reservoir, he lost his balance and slipped over the edge to his death.

People who visit the reservoir have claimed to see an apparition of a younger man staggering near the edge of the Holiday Creek Reservoir before falling over. Sometimes the sound of breaking glass can be heard accompanying the apparition. It is believed that the sound of the breaking glass is actually the sound of his liquor bottle breaking as it hits the ground right before Tom falls into the reservoir.

Fort Worth

....

Log Cabin Village

2100 Log Cabin Village Lane

The Log Cabin Village was a preservation project supervised by the Pioneer Texas Heritage Committee to ensure that the lifestyle of early settlers and residents of northern Texas would not be forgotten. From the 1950s until 2004, the Log Cabin Village acquired six cabins that exhibited the different architectural styles that were used in northern Texas.

Each of the six cabins was transported from different areas in northern Texas and as such, each has a different history associated with it. In at least two cases, it appears that ghosts were brought along with their respective cabins when they were moved to Log Cabin Village.

The Foster Cabin was built in the 1850s by Henry and Martha Foster. Mrs. Foster died in 1870 and after her death, Henry Foster hired Jane Holt as a caretaker for the cabin and a nanny for his children. Jane loved the smell of lilacs and would often wear lilac-scented perfume when she was working for Henry Foster. It is believed that the ghost of June Holt haunts Foster Cabin because people who visit the cabin will often notice the scent of lilacs in the building all throughout the year. Also, people who have gone on tours of the Foster Cabin have heard the sound of people walking on the second floor even though it is vacant.

A second cabin that is haunted at Log Cabin Village involves a man who may have been hanged. In the first-floor room of the second cabin, people often hear a door loudly slamming, although the source for the sound is never found. There have also been several claims that the apparition of a man will sometimes accompany the sound of the slamming door. The man is described as in his thirties with dark hair, but the most disturbing feature is that his neck appears to be broken as if he had been hanged. It could be that this is the ghost of a man who had been hanged where this cabin originally stood and that it simply came along when the cabin was relocated to Log Cabin Village.

Dallas

Buckner Orphans' Home

On January 16, 1897, one of the worst fires in Dallas's history broke out in the boys' dormitory of the Buckner Orphans' Home, located about a mile north of the old Texas and Pacific Railroad station. Unlike the girls' dormitory, which was made primarily from stone and brick, the boys' dormitory was an older structure made primarily of wood. At the time of the fire, the dormitory housed about 110 orphaned boys.

The fire started about 10:00 p.m., January 16, 1897, on the first floor. According to newspaper reports, the fire burned so hot that a search for victims could not begin until the following morning after the blaze had been extinguished.

A total of fifteen boys ranging from six to seventeen years of age died in the fire or as a result of burns. Three of the bodies were so burned that officials could not identify them, other than to say they were residents of the orphanage.

The fire was discovered by Sallie Britton, the dormitory matron. She had been sleeping with her four children for warmth on that January morning. She awoke to the smell of smoke, and when she got up to investigate the source, she realized that the floor was very hot to the touch. She immediately ran out of her room to warn the boys in their rooms. After alerting the boys, she returned to her own room to ensure that her own children were safe. She returned just in time to see the floor of her bedroom collapse, taking the bed and three of her four children with it to their deaths. Her oldest daughter had managed to escape through the bedroom window. She had attempted to wake her siblings, and thought they had followed her out the window. Only later did she realize that she was the only one of Sallie Britton's children to survive.

According to the *Galveston Daily News*, after the fire was extinguished and the bodies were gathered together, the older boys that escaped from the fire built pine coffins for the fifteen boys who perished in the fire. They were buried by 4:00 p.m., January 17, 1897, in the orphanage cemetery behind the dormitories in a light rain.

There are those who say that the area where the dormitory stood and the nearby cemetery is haunted by the boys who lost their lives on January 16, 1897. Sometimes the unexplained strong smell of burning wood can be noticed at this location. Also, in the cemetery where the orphans were buried, the sounds of crying can be heard.

San Angelo

Fort Concho
630 South Oakes Street

Much like nearby Fort Richardson, Fort Concho was originally built to protect settlers and their families while the area was growing into a viable community. Unlike Fort Richardson, which was named after a fallen general, Fort Concho is named for the nearby Concho River.

Built in 1867, Fort Concho was actively used for twenty-two years, until it was decommissioned on June 20, 1889. While in operation, Fort Concho was crucial to the formation of San Angelo, Texas. In addition to protecting the settlers, the fort eventually became a frequent stagecoach stop and was one of the first places in the area that received mail.

Fort Concho had nearly forty buildings spread out over forty acres of land. After Fort Concho was abandoned in 1889, the buildings went into disrepair. Of the forty original buildings, only twenty-three were able to be saved. The remaining seventeen buildings were carefully reconstructed when Fort Concho became a National Historic Landmark in 1961.

After the fort was opened to the public, people started to notice ghostly activity in some of the buildings. Three areas of Fort Concho are haunted: the fort headquarters, the officers' living quarters, and the fort chapel.

The fort headquarters is apparently haunted by an active serviceman named Second Sergeant James Cunningham. He was the only casualty recorded while Fort Concho was in active service. He did not die during an attack on the fort or in battle, but rather he was a victim of the bottle. Cunningham was a severe alcoholic and, due to years of drinking, his liver had been nearly destroyed by cirrhosis. After speaking with a doctor about his condition, he was given the bad news that he did not have much longer to live. Knowing that his days were numbered, Cunningham requested that he spend his last days at the Fort Concho headquarters so that he could be with his colleagues and friends when he died. About six weeks later, Cunningham died in his sleep.

After Fort Concho opened to the public as a national historic landmark, a uniformed soldier has been seen walking near the old fort headquarters, which had been converted into a museum. Besides walking toward the headquarters, his form is sometimes seen inside the windows after the museum has closed. In most cases, the apparition appears for only a few seconds before disappearing, but sometimes the smell of liquor accompanies the appearance. As the only ghost associated with headquarters, it can be assumed to be the ghost of James Cunningham.

A second area of Fort Concho that is haunted is known as Officers' Row, which has at least two ghosts associated with it. Officers' Row was a series of stone buildings that served as the homes for the officers and their families. The regimental commander of the 10th Calvary was a man named Benjamin Grierson, who lived in Officers' Row with his family, including his young daughter, Edith.

When Edith was almost twelve years old, she became severely ill and died. The bedroom where Edith died is usually much colder than the rest of the building. An apparition of a young girl can often be seen sitting on the floor playing jacks. Edith's ghost appears oblivious to the people who enter the room, but it will disappear if a person stays for any length of time.

A second ghost associated with Officers' Row is that of Colonel Ranald MacKenzie, the commanding officer at Fort Concho when it was decommissioned in June 1889. While most people stationed at the fort moved on with their lives, Colonel MacKenzie opted to stay at Fort Concho until his death several years later. Since Mackenzie's death, his ghost has been seen at his old residence at Officers' Row. Most ghost hunters who have investigated this site agree that Mackenzie's ghost is the most active haunting at Fort Concho. Mackenzie was known for constantly cracking his knuckles and incessant pacing, especially when he was worried or deep in thought. The sound of cracking knuckles and heavy, pacing footsteps have been heard in his old residence in Officers' Row and have been recorded as EVPs by ghost hunters who have investigated the fort.

The third haunted building at Fort Concho is the fort's chapel. George Dunbar was the chaplain at Fort Concho. Dunbar was described as a very devout chaplain, loving husband, and dedicated father to his six children, who stayed at the fort with him. While serving at Fort Concho, Chaplain Dunbar was transferred to nearby Fort Sill. While at Fort Sill, Dunbar often talked of his family and his desire to be reunited with them at Fort Concho. However, while stationed at Fort Sill, Dunbar was killed in a Comanche attack against the fort. His body was returned to Fort Concho and claimed by his widow. Dunbar was known to be a very passionate and animated chaplain, and his voice was heard throughout the entire fort when he was delivering a sermon. Today, people who visit Fort Concho can still hear the loud and powerful voice of Chaplain George Dunbar giving a sermon. There have also been several sightings of a man in Union uniform standing or kneeling in prayer inside of the chapel. When the chapel is photographed by visitors, it is not uncommon for the photo to be filled with bluish-white orbs. These orbs usually do not appear in photographs of other areas of the fort.

Texarkana

....

Moonlight Murders
North Park Road

Texarkana is an interesting little town that is partly located in both the states of Texas and Arkansas. This quiet town was also the site of one of the nation's most heinous killing sprees that took place in the 1940s and remains unsolved to this day.

In 1946, Texarkana and surrounding communities were the target of a mass killer who has become known to locals and the media as the Phantom Killer or the Moonlight Murderer. In a four-month period between February and May 1946, a series of attacks led to the deaths of at least seven people. The killing spree soon became known as the Moonlight Murders because the killer only attacked his victims at night.

Two of the Phantom Killer's victims were Paul Martin and Betty Jo Booker. Betty Jo was a talented saxophone player and had finished playing at the local VFW club about 1:30 a.m., Sunday, April 14, 1946. Her life friend, Paul Martin, had agreed to take her home after the show, but they never arrived. After family members became worried about their absence, they started to search for the couple. They found Paul between 6:30 and 7:00 a.m. on North Park Road near Spring Lake Park. He had been shot twice in the head, once in the right hand, and once through his left ribs with a .32 caliber pistol. Betty Jo's body was found around 11:30 a.m. about two miles from where the body of her friend was discovered a few hours before. She had been shot in the face and once in the left side with the same gun.

Over the next four months, five other people were murdered in a similar fashion by the Phantom Killer. Of all the victims, only three survived their ordeal. The only description of the attacker provided by one of the survivors was that he was at least six feet tall with a very large build. His identity was concealed by a white bag covering his head with two holes for the eyes and one hole for the mouth.

The final victim of the Phantom Killer of Texarkana was Earl McSpadden. His body was found along the railroad tracks just north of Texarkana. Unlike most of the other murders, McSpadden had been stabbed rather than shot. After McSpadden's murder, the killings stopped just as unexpectedly as they had started four months earlier. Although there were leads as to the true identity of the Phantom Killer, he was never captured and the murders remain unsolved to this day.

There are three ghost stories associated with the Moonlight Murders of Texarkana. The first story takes place where Betty Jo Booker's body was discovered on North Park Road. Over the years there have been reports of a saxophone playing softly in the wind, especially on nights near 1:30 in the morning.

The second story takes place near the entrance to Spring Lake Park where Paul Martin's car was located. At times, there have been sightings of a 1940s vehicle parked alongside the road that vanishes when approached. Some have even reported hearing a series of four gunshots near the area.

The final story appears to be of the Phantom Killer's final victim, Earl McSpadden. Since 1946, the apparition of a man fitting Earl McSpadden's description has been seen walking along the railroad tracks near where his body was discovered.

SIX

NEW MEXICO

---

487 miles

O f the eight states that Route 66 goes through, the state that had the longest stretch of the Mother Road was New Mexico, with 487 miles. Although much of the actual route is no longer accessible by anything other than a four-wheel drive vehicle, that doesn't change the fact that New Mexico has a special place in the hearts of those adventurous enough to travel the entire length of Route 66.

When people think of the paranormal in regard to New Mexico, the famous Roswell crash incident of 1947 comes to mind. However, it is certainly not the only paranormal event that has taken place in the "Land of Enchantment." There have been hundreds of ghost sightings here that reflect the area's Native American and Spanish influence as well as the sacrifices

that the miners and railroad workers made to make New Mexico the wonderful state that it is today.

Madrid

....

Madrid was founded in the 1850s as a small company-owned coal mining town by the Albuquerque and Cerrillos Coal Company. The town began to grow because of the coal industry and by 1899, it had approximately 2,500 residents. It was a fairly prosperous town as long as there was coal to be mined from the nearby Ortiz Mountains. However, in the 1950s, the mines were forced to close and many people who worked for the coal company found themselves unemployed. A few businesses tried to stay open after the miners and their families left, but as the remaining residents moved away, they closed as well. Madrid was well on its way to becoming just another ghost town.

For nearly twenty years, most of the buildings in Madrid were vacant and left to deteriorate. However, in the early 1970s, Madrid was given an opportunity that most ghost towns along Route 66 never had. Several of the buildings had been vacant for years and the property was being sold for prices much lower than the estimated market value.

This did not escape the notice of several hippies and other members of America's counterculture of the early 1970s. A group of individuals pooled their resources and purchased a considerable portion of the town of Madrid. The fact that Madrid was somewhat isolated was an added bonus for the new owners. After a lot of hard work, Madrid was resurrected and is once again on the map with a population of nearly four hundred residents. The town has boutiques, coffee shops, museums, and other businesses and events all year long that cater to the artisans, craftsmen, and other creative folk. Of course, there also just happens to be a few ghosts lingering around as well.

Mine Shaft Tavern
2846 Highway 14

The Mine Shaft Tavern was the bar where many of the miners gathered for the last time when it was announced in 1954 that the mines were going to be closed down permanently. The original Mine Shaft Tavern burned down on Christmas Day in 1944, but was rebuilt in 1947 on the same spot and has been there to this day. It has been the on-site locations for several movies, including *Wild Hogs* and *Paul*.

The ghostly activity associated with the Mine Shaft Tavern goes back to the days of the miners. Most of the activity at the Mine Shaft Tavern includes physical manifestations, such as doors opening and closing by themselves, glasses and dinnerware in the kitchen falling onto the floor, and lights turning on and off by themselves. There is one story associated with one of the mirrors in the bar. If a person looks into the mirror at the bar, they can sometimes see the reflection of another person staring back at them or look at them over their shoulder. It is believed to be the ghost of one of the miners who did not want to leave the area when the mines closed in the 1950s.

Old Madrid Cemetery

The old Madrid Cemetery is where a great deal of the ghost sightings in the town takes place. Most of the people were buried here when it was the mining town owned by the Albuquerque and Cerrillos Coal Company. Although nobody has been buried in old Madrid Cemetery for decades, the apparitions of the miners who once lived in Madrid have been seen walking among the tombstones. Even though these ghosts are seen on a fairly regular basis, none of the apparitions have been positively identified.

Madrid Church

When people started to purchase buildings and properties in Madrid in the early 1970s, one person bought a church that had been standing in Madrid for several years and converted it into a private residence. Visitors claim to hear loud church bells late at night, although the bells were removed several years ago. The sounds of people singing hymns have also been heard by those who have stayed at the house overnight.

Madrid Mine Collapse

Several years before the coal mines were closed in Madrid, there was an explosion in the Morgan Jones mine in December 1932 that killed fourteen men. The bodies were all removed from the Morgan Jones Mine and buried in the old Madrid Cemetery. There are nights when people have been able to hear the miners' pleas for help from beneath the remains of the collapsed mine shaft.

La Llorona

Another local legend that has become associated with Madrid is that of La Llorona. Since dozens of towns have their own version of this story, it is likely more of an urban legend rather than a real haunting. Madrid's version of La Llorona is that in the surrounding arroyos, or dry creek beds, there is the spirit of a grieving woman who drowned her children and is now cursed to wander the arroyos for eternity as punishment for her crime. She can be seen as a ghostly white light wandering through the dry creek beds near Madrid. Sometimes her voice can be heard on the wind, calling for her children to come back to her.

Mexican Señorita

Another haunting that Madrid has become famous for is that of a beautiful Mexican señorita who has been seen walking down the main street of the town. She is described as a woman in her early twenties with dark brown eyes and flowing shoulder-length black hair, wearing a long floral dress. Her ghost is sometimes accompanied by a tall cowboy walking by her side.

Santa Fe

....

Grant Corner Inn

122 Grant Ave

The Grant Corner Inn was originally built as a three-story private residence in 1905 by a young newlywed couple that moved to Santa Fe from another part of the United States. Within a few years after moving into the house, the husband died, which left the wife to take care of their infant son alone.

The wife eventually remarried and for a few years she, her son, and her new husband lived in the home in relative happiness. According to most people, her new husband was very demanding and not very nice. The winter after they were married, her son developed a serious health problem and required constant care. She devoted all of her time to taking care of her son, but after about a year, he died.

After her son was buried, the woman and her new husband decided to leave Santa Fe in order to start a new life together. She never returned to the area again.

The house was left vacant for a few years and rumors that the house was haunted began to spread throughout the neighborhood. People who walked by the abandoned house claimed to see a light in the boy's old bedroom late at night, although nobody was living there at the time and there was no electricity connected to the house.

The house eventually was purchased and the new residents almost immediately began to notice that they were not alone. They claimed to have heard loud knocking and the sound of furniture being moved from the boy's old bedroom. When the owners went to check on the sounds and opened the bedroom door, none of the furniture had been moved. This occurred on a regular basis for several years.

The house was again sold to new buyers who renovated it into a ten-room bed-and-breakfast now known as the Grant Corner Inn. After the bed-and-breakfast opened for business, guests began to tell the owners of their own paranormal experiences, which appear to be concentrated in room 4, room 8, and the second-floor hallway leading to the third floor.

Room 4 of the Grant Corner Inn was the room where the boy actually stayed. This is where most of the loud knocking and scrapings have been heard over the years. Room 8 has had objects fall off the shelves and paintings and other wall hangings fall from the walls. In addition, people have heard the sound of a woman crying in this room, which is likely where the mother stayed.

The hallway and staircase leading to the third floor is the only section of the Grant Corner Inn that has had any apparitions to speak of. There have been several reports of a shadowy figure seen walking from the hallway on the second floor to the top of the stairs on the third floor. It is believed that this shadow person is actually the ghost of the first husband, who died in this house a few years after moving into it.

Unfortunately, the Grant Corner Inn closed its doors about four years ago and is no longer in business.

La Posada
330 East Palace Avenue

This three-story bed-and-breakfast was built as a private residence by wealthy businessman Abraham Staab in 1882 and is believed to be the first brick building built in the Santa Fe area. Staab had a considerable amount of money and was known to host elaborate parties for Santa Fe's elite at his home. Some of Staab's party guests included former President Rutherford Hayes, General Sherman, and others. Not only was Staab a Santa Fe socialite, but he and his wife Julie, had a total of seven children together while living at La Posada. However, their youngest son died only a few months after he was born.

The unexpected death of their infant son put an end to the parties the Staabs hosted at La Posada. Julie, usually a very cheerful and outgoing woman, became somewhat of a recluse and sank into a deep depression.

She spent most of her time in the second-floor bedroom where she gave birth to her son and he subsequently died. She died in this bedroom in 1896 when she was fifty-two years old. Some believe that she actually grieved herself to death over the loss of her infant son.

The Staab's home was purchased by R. H. Nason in the 1930s, who transformed it into a hotel by adding several additional buildings near the original mansion and carriage house. Nason named his new business venture La Posada, which translates to "resting place" in Spanish. Since then, La Posada has become well-known throughout the southwestern United States for its hospitality and fine food.

However, guests staying in room 256 at La Posada might have an experience different than most of the others. When the Staabs owned the mansion, room 256 was Julie's bedroom, which is where she and her infant son died. Many guests who have stayed in this room believe that Julie's restless spirit is still felt here.

Room 256 has exhibited some rather dramatic poltergeist activity. Guests have frequently been awakened from sleep by the loud sound of rushing water. When trying to find the source, they discover that all of the bathroom faucets have been turned on. Also, many guests have complained that this room is much colder than the rest of the building. On one occasion, there was a report of a maintenance man knocking on the door to make certain the room was closed when he heard somebody say, "Come in." Surprised to hear somebody reply to his knock, the maintenance man went inside only to find that the room was empty.

Groundskeepers and other guests have seen a sad-looking woman watching them through the window of room 256 even if that room is vacant at the time of the sighting. The woman seen looking out the window has been identified as Julie Staab when they see a portrait of her hanging in the La Posada sitting room on the first floor.

Although most of the ghostly activity at La Posada takes place in room 256, Julie has also been seen in other parts of the original mansion. Her apparition has been seen wandering the hallways of the first and second floors near room 256. She has also been seen walking up the stairway leading from the second floor to the third floor of the mansion, which was where the Staabs held most of the parties. Generally, she is seen wearing a white dress, although when her apparition is seen near Room 256, she is wearing a black dress.

Laguna Pueblo Mission

The Laguna Pueblo Mission is one of the oldest churches in Santa Fe. It was the sight of an Indian attack in 1733 in which Father Juan Padilla was brutally murdered. Survivors of the attack made a makeshift coffin from a cottonwood tree and buried him in a place where his body could never be desecrated—inside the church itself. The floorboards in front of the main altar were pulled up and a grave was dug for Father Padilla's coffin. There the father's corpse rested in relative peace for twenty years. However, in 1753, the coffin worked its way up and broke through the floorboards. Father Padilla's coffin was buried in the same spot again and the floorboards were replaced. His coffin remained undisturbed for more than a century. However, in 1889, Father Padilla's coffin once again arose from its grave and broke through the floorboards. Again, the parishioners at the Laguna Pueblo Mission buried their beloved father in the same spot in front of the altar. Twenty-five years later, on Christmas Eve in 1914, the coffin once again came to the surface. At this point, the coffin was buried outside of the church, and there have been no reports of it arising to the surface since then.

San Miguel Mission

401 Old Santa Fe Trail

The Mission of San Miguel is the oldest church in the United States that is still in use today. It was built between the years of 1610 and 1626. In the Pueblos Revolt of 1680, San Miguel Mission was moderately damaged, but it was repaired in 1710 to be used as a church for the Spanish soldiers that were in the area.

Although this story is not actually a ghost story per se, it does involve the paranormal or quite possibly the miraculous. The story goes that the San Jose Bell was brought from Spain and placed at the Mission of San Miguel in the mid-1800s.

According to the story, one patron at the mission was a blind man who was a very devout Christian. He prayed at the mission every day for years. One day, the San Jose Bell began to ring by itself while the blind man was praying. While it was ringing, the man, who had been blind from birth, could see his surroundings. After a short time, the bell stopped ringing and the man once again could no longer see. When asked by the priest and other parishioners to describe the surroundings, he did so accurately. This was apparently the only miracle associated with the bell, which still stands on display at the mission today.

In the gift shop is the only ghost truly associated with the mission. It is reportedly a ghost of a little boy who died in the 1940s. According to people who have encountered him, the boy is friendly and does not cause any problems. He simply makes his presence as a shadowy apparition.

La Casa Vieja de Analco
215 East de Vargas Street

Across the street from the rear section of the Mission of San Miguel, the oldest church in the United States, stands the oldest house in the United States. This house and the surrounding street have a few ghost stories associated with it. The most well-known story is of a soldier in the Spanish Army and his involvement with two *brujas*, or witches, who reportedly lived in this house in the late 1600s.

In 1675, Governor Juan Francisco Treviño arrested nearly fifty Pueblo shamans for practicing witchcraft and ordered their public execution by hanging. Only three of the shamans were actually put to death, but their deaths and subsequent poor treatment of the Pueblo shamans eventually set the stage for the Pueblo Revolt of 1680. Since then, many people who were not captured by Treviño kept their shamanic and other religious practices very private.

In the late 1680s, shortly after the Pueblo Revolt in 1680, Juan Treviño met and fell in love with one of the local women. The two began to see each other every day, and after a few months, Juan proposed to her. He was shocked when she refused his proposal because she was also seeing another man. The other man had already proposed and she had already agreed to give him her hand in marriage. Desperate to keep the woman's love for himself, Juan did something completely unthinkable for an officer in the Spanish Army in the 1600s after the Pueblo Revolt…he sought out the help of two brujas who lived at La Casa Vieja de Analco. Initially, they were skeptical of the soldier's request, fearing that it was a trap that would expose them as witches. However, after convincing them that his intentions were sincere, the brujas agreed to help. They prepared a love potion and gave it to Juan, guaranteeing that the mixture would give him the heart of the woman he loved.

Juan followed the directions the brujas had given to him, but the potion did not work as promised because the woman married the other man. Infuriated, Juan confronted the brujas and demanded a refund. The brujas refused to give Juan his money back, so he drew his sword from his scabbard and tried to attack the two women. In the fight that followed, one of the witches tripped Juan, causing him to lose his balance. One of the brujas took his sword and, in a move that would make any Highlander proud, decapitated Juan in one quick motion. They made certain that when Juan was buried, his body was not buried with his decapitated head because this would ensure that his spirit would never be at rest. The brujas then hid Juan's head before arranging to have his body found by some of his colleagues in the Spanish Army.

On cool spring nights in this part of Santa Fe, a headless Spanish soldier can be seen wandering down the streets near La Casa Vieja de

Analco. Some say that it is Juan searching for his missing head so that he can finally be at peace, while others believe that he is simply looking for the two brujas in order to get revenge.

Albuquerque

Maria Teresa Restaurant
614 Rio Grande NW

The Maria Teresa Restaurant was originally built as a private residence, or hacienda, by Salvador Armijo sometime between the late 1780s and mid-1830s. The hacienda was eventually converted into the Maria Teresa Restaurant, which operated for several years. However, the restaurant has been closed since 2004. There are at least five separate ghosts that have been identified at the Maria Teresa Restaurant, which may make it one of the most haunted places in New Mexico.

The most famous ghost at the Maria Teresa Restaurant was named Maria by the employees and regulars. She has been described as a young Hispanic woman with her long hair pulled back. Maria appears to be very fond of small children and can sometimes be seen by them rather than by adults. She is usually found only in one of the restaurant's three dining rooms.

A second ghost that has been seen throughout the entire restaurant is that of an older man wearing a dark outfit. This man usually makes himself known by being seen only in one of the restaurant's many mirrors. Customers have claimed to see not only their own reflection, but also that of this older man standing behind them. When they turn around, they are usually surprised that there is nobody standing behind them. Some believe that this older gentleman is none other than Salvador Armijo himself.

There are three dining rooms in the Maria Teresa Restaurant that are said to be where most of the ghosts can be found. Along the far wall of the Armijo Room is an old piano that can sometimes be heard playing by itself long after the restaurant and dining room are closed for the evening. Sometimes, the sounds of laughter and singing can also be heard from this room when it is empty.

The Chacon Room is another dining room that is known to be haunted by the ghost of a well-groomed younger man dressed in expensive black clothing. Before the restaurant closed, some customers confused him with an employee. When the customers attempted to speak with this young man, his apparition would sometimes disappear right in front of them. It is not known who this ghost could have been when he was alive.

The Sarachino Room is the final dining room that is haunted. This dining room's ghost is described as a middle-aged woman with dark hair, wearing a red dress. Sometimes, the faint smell of perfume will accompany the apparition of this woman. She is believed to be one of the daughters of Salvador Armijo.

Although each dining room appears to have a distinct ghost associated with it, all three have experienced typical poltergeist activity such as silverware and place settings that would disappear prior to the restaurant opening.

Kimo Theater
423 Central Ave. NW

The Kimo Theater opened its doors to the public on September 19, 1927. The owner, Oreste Bachechi, had always wanted to open a theater for the residents of Albuquerque. Investing $150,000 of his own money, Bachechi opened the theater, which instantly became a great success. The state-of-the-art theater had a movie projector for the silent films of the day, a separate stage for live performances, a 700-seat auditorium, balconies, and several other amenities for both the audience and performers. The reputation of the Kimo spread, and soon big-name celebrities such as Ginger Rogers started to perform there on a regular basis.

The Kimo offered all sorts of attractions for twenty-four years without incident. However, in 1951, a tragic accident occurred that would change the Kimo Theater forever. Six-year-old Bobby Darnell was watching a movie with some friends in the upper balcony. He suddenly stood up and left the balcony in a hurry. Whether he got scared by a scene in the movie or just wanted to get a drink from the concession stand will never be known. Just as he was running down the stairs from the balcony to the lobby, a boiler exploded in the basement, which destroyed part of the lobby and the staircase that Bobby Darnell was descending, killing him instantly.

The Kimo was closed for several weeks in order to repair the damage to the lobby and the staircase. When the Kimo reopened, people soon started to see a little boy wearing jeans and a striped shirt playing on the staircase or in the balcony where Bobby had been sitting in just prior to the explosion.

Over the years, a tradition of sorts was started by performers at the Kimo Theater. When a performance was first being rehearsed, cast members would tie doughnuts to a pipe along the wall backstage as a token of luck for a successful performance. Performers believe that if they do not pay this tribute of respect to Bobby, he will trip them during rehearsal and cause problems during a performance.

A second ghost has been known to haunt the Kimo Theater. A woman wearing a long dress and bonnet has appeared walking the halls and down one of the aisles of the main auditorium. Nobody knows who this woman is, and it appears that she is oblivious to her surroundings and is seen much more infrequently than the ghost of Bobby Darnell.

Haunted Hill
Menaul Boulevard
Residents in the Menaul Boulevard neighborhood of Albuquerque know that the hills in the distance are haunted. They say that when people walk among the foothills after sunset or after dark, they can often hear screaming in the distance, laughing up close to a person's ears, or the echo of gunshots. There are some caves among the foothills beyond Menaul

Boulevard that people rarely go to because they believe that it is also haunted. Locals claim that one cave in particular has the ghost of an older man with a weathered face sitting in the cave entrance with a lantern on the ground beside him. The light can be seen for over a mile away, but when anybody is brave enough to investigate the light, it can never be found and the cave mouth is always empty.

Corralles

Rancho de Corralles

This restaurant was originally a private hacienda (estate) built in 1801 by Diego Montoya. The house and surrounding property was very serene for several years. However, that would soon change.

The hacienda was sold to Luis and Louisa Emberto in 1883. It has been said that their relationship had been very volatile at times, often erupting into physical confrontations and rumors of infidelity from both parties. Although this was the case, the Emberto's were known to host very exquisite and expensive dinner parties for their frequent guests.

Their ultimate undoing began at one of these parties five years after purchasing the property. During one of the parties, Sr. and Sra. Emberto's son publicly accused his father of having an affair with one of the female guests present. The son was so adamant that his father's infidelity was tearing apart the family that he killed the woman at the party in front of all the guests.

Luis became enraged at his son and his wife. Luis believed that his wife had told her son of the affair and actually encouraged him to kill the woman to humiliate him in front of his guests. Shortly after the incident, Luis moved out of the hacienda. Before he left for the final time, he walked up to Louisa and threatened to return one day to kill her and her lover.

Sixteen years had passed and nobody had heard from Luis Emberto. One night in 1898, Luis returned to the hacienda unexpectedly. Although things had been quiet for several years and Louisa in fact had several lovers after Luis left, she was always prepared for her husband's return. Even while she slept, Louisa was always armed with a pistol. When Luis confronted Louisa, she attempted to shoot him, but he fired first. The first shot severely injured Louisa, and with a second shot at close range, Luis made certain that his wife was indeed dead.

Soon after the shooting, an armed posse found Luis in hiding and surrounded him. They attempted to take him in for the murder of his wife, but Luis refused to surrender. A shootout commenced and by the time it was over, Luis Emberto had been killed.

Luis's body was taken back to the hacienda and preparations for burial of both bodies were being made. However, because of the events surrounding their marital indiscretions and their respective deaths, neither was allowed to be buried in the town's cemetery. It was decided that the couple was to be buried beside one another on the west side of the hacienda near an irrigation ditch. Their bodies remain there to this day.

Due to the violent nature of the deaths at Rancho de Corrales, there is naturally a lot of spiritual energy at the hacienda. There is an apparition that is believed to be the ghost of Louisa Emberto. She has long dark brown hair and is wearing a long flowing white dress. Sometimes she is seen in the bar and in other places in the hacienda. She has also been known to appear at her and her husband's gravesite.

Other activity at the Rancho de Corrales includes dining room furniture rearranging itself after the restaurant is closed. Other times, the bathroom water faucets will be found running in the morning, although they had been turned off the night before.

There also appears to be the sound of loud parties in the area where the Emberto's hosted their lavish dinner parties. Late at night, long after the restaurant has closed, people have reported hearing the loud sounds of a man and woman quarreling. At times, the sound of arguing comes from what was once Louisa's bedroom and at other times it can be heard near the gravesites.

Los Lunas

······················

Luna-Otero Mansion

110 W. Main Street

What would become known as the Luna-Otero dynasty began in the 1690s when the King of Spain granted a man by the name of Domingo de Luna a vast parcel of land in the area now known as Los Lunas, New Mexico.

Not long after Domingo de Luna began to expand his fortune by raising livestock and purchasing surrounding property, Don Pedro Otero was also given neighobring land by the King of Spain. Otero also became very wealthy and soon had a fortune. Rather than being rivals, the Luna and Otero families were very friendly and merged their wealth and resources through the marriages of Manuel Otero to Eloisa Luna on June 2, 1879, and Salomon Luna to Adeliada Otero on January 15, 1882. After the marriages, the family became known as the Luna-Oteros. In addition to their vast political influence and wealth, the families had over 30,000 acres of land.

In the late 1870s, the Santa Fe Railroad Company approached Antonio Luna for permission to put a long stretch of railroad on the Luna property in order to expand westward. Taking advantage of the opportunity, Antonio Luna agreed to this only if the Santa Fe Railroad Company would build a mansion for him. The colonial-style mansion was completed in 1881, the same year that Antonio died.

The Luna-Otero mansion and was left virtually unchanged until the early twentieth century. In the 1920s, Eduardo Otero and his wife Josefita made several renovations to the Luna-Otero mansion including adding a solarium, a portico, and a large wrought-iron fence that surrounded the mansion proper. These changes can be seen at the mansion to this day. The mansion has passed hands several times over the years, and opened as a restaurant in the 1970s. After converting the mansion into an upscale restaurant, there has been a great deal of paranormal activity reported at the Luna-Otero Mansion.

Josefita's second-floor bedroom, which is now a lounge, is where most of the paranormal activity occurs. A woman fitting Josefita Luna-Otero's description has been seen looking out the lounge's second-floor window. Witnesses describe Josefita as a quiet, pleasant-looking woman with her hair pulled back and wearing a white button-down blouse from the late 1920s and early 1930s. There is an uncanny resemblance between the apparition and an old photograph found of Josefita. Some who have seen Josefita looking out the window get the impression that she is either waiting for somebody to arrive or simply watching passersby.

On more than one occasion, a waitress has attempted to take an order from a woman sitting in a chair looking out the window. If the waitress turns her head for just a moment, the apparition always disappears. This has also happened to lounge patrons who have wanted to strike up a conversation with Josefita. Also, Josefita's ghost has frequently been seen on the staircase leading from the ground floor to the second floor of the mansion.

The second floor and the staircase of the Luna-Otero Mansion are not the only places to have ghostly activity. On the first floor, reports of the apparitions of two people dressed in period clothing resembling servants appear to be in a hushed conversation are not uncommon. Sometimes the apparitions will only be seen and on other occasions, only the sounds of two people whispering can be heard. All attempts to try to decipher what the whispering voices are saying end in failure. However, sometimes the apparitions and the voices can be experienced together.

In addition to the three ghosts that frequent the Luna-Otero Mansion, there is the typical poltergeist activity often associated with hauntings. Doors have been known to open and lose by themselves, objects have been known to disappear and then reappear later, and glassware has been known to shatter for no apparent reason. This poltergeist activity can be experienced on both the first and second floors of the Luna-Otero Mansion.

Los Lunas Mystery Stone

Not far from the Luna Mansion is one of the most interesting ancient enigmas that has been found in New Mexico or any other part of the western United States. The Los Lunas Mystery Stone was discovered in the 1880s by a boy who was wandering in the wilderness behind his home. It was brought to the attention of archaeologist Frank Hibben from the University of New Mexico. Hibben first wrote about the mystery stone in 1933, and it has been a hotly debated topic ever since.

The stone weighs approximately eighty tons and appears to have an ancient text carved onto a flat side of the stone. According to some interpretations, the text appears to be an abridged version of the Ten Commandments written in ancient Hebrew. Others believe it to be an account of a Roman and appears to be anywhere between 500 and 2,000 years old. Some archaeologists believe it to be a marker left behind by the lost tribe of Israel. Some even believe that it was written by one of the area's first Spanish settlers.

No matter what the text can be interpreted as, there is even more controversy involving the age of the stone. Some experts feel that the stone was likely created in the late 1880s by a local who wanted to put Los Lunas on the map. Others believe that the stone is authentic and offers credence to the theory that the area was visited by a lost tribe of Israel who made it to the United States and eventually New Mexico several hundred years ago.

In regards to any paranormal activity, there have not been any apparitions or poltergeist activity associated with the Los Lunas Mystery Stone. However, there have been small, bright lights seen near the stone that cannot be explained. In years past, there seems to be evidence that pagan rituals were conducted at the site and offerings were sometimes placed at the base of the stone. In recent years, this activity has stopped because the stone can only be viewed by paying $25 for a permit from the New Mexico State Land Office.

SEVEN

ARIZONA

---

401 miles

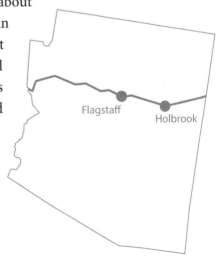

The natural beauty of Arizona is breathtaking, and the land itself is steeped in history that goes back hundreds, if not thousands, of years. If you would ask locals their opinion of the most significant events of the state's past, some would talk about the towns that sprang up over night in response to the railroads and mines that signified the industrial and technological taming of the rugged countryside. Others will tell you about how the land is filled with the spirits of their ancestors who watch over them and may sometimes influence current events. Perhaps both are correct in some regard and Route 66 is a unique merger of both the archetypes of industry and spirit.

155

Holbrook

....

Navajo County Historic Courthouse

100 East Arizona Avenue

The Navajo County Historic Courthouse was constructed in 1898 and served as the courthouse and jail for Holbrook and surrounding communities up until 1976. Today, the courthouse building is home to the Holbrook Chamber of Commerce and local Historical Society.

Being the center of government for nearly eighty years, the courthouse has seen its share of trials. However, there was only one man that was executed by public hanging during that time. The unlucky recipient of that honor was a man by the name of George Smiley.

George Smiley was arrested in November 1899 for the murder of a railroad employee by the name of Mr. McSweeney. Apparently, Smiley was working under McSweeney for the Santa Fe Railroad Company. Smiley had worked extra hours and was owed some back pay. However, before Smiley could collect his pay, McSweeney quit his job as foreman. Smiley went to the new foreman about his back pay, but said there was no documentation of the extra work and to take it up with McSweeney.

Smiley confronted McSweeney the next day, who stated that had quit and was no longer involved with any of the the Santa Fe Railroad's dealings. After going back and forth several times between the new foreman and McSweeney, George Smile got drunk at a local saloon. He saw McSweeny outside and confronted him once again about his lost wages. Realizing that Smiley was drunk, McSweeney turned to walk away. At that point, Smiley fired two shots into McSweeney's back and killed him. There were several witnesses, and all pointed out that Smiley had shot McSweeney while unarmed and with his back turned.

Smiley was arrested for McSweeney's murder and convicted on October 14, 1899. The verdict was that Smiley was to be executed by hanging in front of the courthouse at 2:00 p.m., December 8, 1899.

Because of the revised Statutes of Arizona Penal Codes, Title X, Section 1849, the sheriff was required to prepare and send invitations of the execution to a variety of people, including a physician to confirm the time of death, twelve reputable residents, and the local district attorney. Sheriff Frank Wattron put together an invitation that he felt would capture the attention of those who needed to be present. The invitation indeed caught their attention, but also caught the attention of the Arizona governor and even the President of the United States. The invitation would also make Wattron's name be forever remembered in Holbrook's history. The text of Wattron's invitation read as follows:

> *You are hereby cordially invited to attend the hanging of George Smiley, Murderer. His soul will be swung into eternity on December 8, 1899 at 2 o'clock p.m., sharp. Latest improved methods in the art of scientific strangulation will be employed and everything possible will be done to make the proceedings cheerful and the execution a success. F. J. Wattron, Sheriff of Navajo County.*

Sheriff Wattron had at least fifty invitations printed for Smiley's execution and sent them to various citizens and politicians. People who had seen the invitation said that it looked and sounded more like a wedding invitation than an announcement for an execution.

Word soon got out about the invitations. Church groups and some individuals began to complain to the Arizona governor Nathan Murphy and even to President William McKinley about the callousness of the invitation's wording. McKinley personally ordered Governor Murphy to take care of the problem for fear that tempers may soon get out of hand. Governor Murphy gave a thirty-day stay of execution for George Smiley and ordered that Sheriff Wattron put together a more conservative and professional invitation. Reluctantly, Wattron redesigned the invitation as requested and sent it to Governor Murphy and several other individuals in the community. The new invitation used some of the wording that Governor Murphy had used in his condemnation of Sheriff Watteron's original invitation. Governor Murphy's invitation also included a request for the state legislature to come up with a template for future execution invitations. The new invitation read:

> *With feelings of profound sorrow and regret, I hereby invite you to attend the private, decent, and humane execution of a human being; name, George Smiley; crime, murder. The said George Smiley will be executed on January 8, 1900 at 2 o'clock p.m. You are expected to deport yourself in a respectable manner, and any "flippant" or "unseemly" language or conduct on your part will not be allowed. Conduct, on anyone's part, bordering on ribaldry and tending to mar the solemnity of the occasion will not be tolerated. F. J. Wattron, Sheriff of Navajo County.*

On January 8, 1900, Smiley's luck had run out. He was hanged at 2:00 p.m. and declared dead eighteen minutes later. The sheriff's actions regarding the invitation may have been the main reason that there were no further executions at the Navajo County Historical Courthouse.

Today, many visitors and employees of the Historical Society and the Chamber of Commerce believe that two or three ghosts haunt the old courthouse. One of the most active ghosts today is that of George Smiley himself. People have seen a man that fits Smiley's description sitting in the cell where he spent his final days. Others have seen a shadowy figure in the doorway on the first floor. Also, items that were in plain sight will disappear only to be found in another location weeks later.

Although George Smiley's ghost may be the most active ghost at the courthouse, he is not the only one to haunt it. People who have driven by the courthouse late at night have seen a light on the second floor. Some claim to see a woman sitting in the window looking outside toward the large tree on the front lawn. They all describe this woman describe her in much the same way. Her expression appears to be very sad. She is described as wearing a dark dress and has long shoulder-length light brown hair. It may be that she is looking out over the site where George Smiley was executed. Although her true identity is unknown, locals have started to call the apparition "Mary." A few historians who are familiar with the courthouse believe that Mary may have been in jail at the same time that George Smiley was incarcerated.

Flagstaff

The Museum Club
3404 East Route 66

The Brunswick (photo courtesy Josh Millstein)

Three miles east of downtown Flagstaff is the Museum Club, a great little bar and nightclub that has become synonymous with Route 66. The Museum Club was built in 1931 by taxidermist and hunting enthusiast Dan Eldridge, who built the giant log structure to display his enormous collection of hunting trophies, gun collection, and other related memorabilia. He also had a small taxidermy service, museum, and trading post inside the building. Eldridge had over 30,000 separate items on display in his building, which he referred to as the "world's largest log cabin." Because of the number of stuffed animals inside, the business was nicknamed "the Zoo" by locals and visitors.

After about five years after Eldridge built the cabin, he sold it to local businessman Doc Williams. Williams took advantage of the building's reputation and converted it into a nightclub and bar. Although Williams made considerable renovations, he decided to keep eighty-five of Eldridge's original trophies on the walls of his new nightclub.

The Museum Club was sold to Don and Thorna Scott in 1963, who converted the bar into a country-western dance hall. Don Scott was a musician who had several connections to the country music industry and within a short time performers such as Waylon Jennings and Willie Nelson started to put on live shows at The Museum Club.

Things were going extremely well for the Scotts and the Museum Club. However, that changed one night in 1973. After closing one night, Thorna was walking upstairs to their apartment on the second floor when she slipped and fell down the steps. She had broken her neck and slipped into a coma as a result of her injury. She never awoke from her coma and died a few days later from her injuries.

After his wife's death, Don Scott fell into a deep depression that could not be shaken no matter how much his friends and family tried to help him. Nearly two years after Thorna died, Don was staying in the lobby of the Museum Club after it had closed for the evening. He walked in front of the giant fireplace that had become one of the highlights of the dance hall and committed suicide by shooting himself with a rifle. He was found the next morning.

After Don's suicide, the Museum Club temporarily closed. It was soon sold and opened under new management. Shortly after reopening, employees and patrons of the new Museum Club said that it had a different feel to it. They started to notice things that made them wonder if the ghosts of Thorna and Don Scott were still at the dance hall.

When the Museum Club reopened, the upstairs apartment was used only for storage—nobody lived there. However, people could hear the sound of somebody walking and the sound of furniture or other heavy items being moved on the second floor. On other nights, people in the parking lot could sometimes see a table lamp or similar light from inside the apartment window. However, since the apartment was used for storage, there was no light source that could produce what the patrons in the parking lot have claimed to see. It is believed that the second-floor apartment is haunted by the ghost of Thorna Scott.

Another place where Thorna Scott's ghost has likely been experienced is at the bottom of the stairs where she had her fatal fall. Patrons and staff have seen a woman fitting Thorna's description standing on the back of the stairway.

The large fireplace where Don Scott shot himself also appears to have some ghostly manifestations of its own. Fires in the fireplace have been known to start when nobody is near. Some people have even claimed to have seen Don's ghost standing in front of the fireplace. Also, bartenders and management staff who open the Museum Club have found the liquor and beer completely rearranged and thrown around, although the bottles were in place the night before.

Hotel Monte Vista
100 North San Francisco Street

The Hotel Monte Vista is one of the most famous landmarks in the Flagstaff area. Built in 1926 and opened to the public on January 1, 1927, it has a total of seventy-three rooms and is the tallest building in Flagstaff. The Hotel Monte Vista was particularly popular during the Prohibition era in the early 1930s because it had developed the reputation of being one of the finest speakeasys in the entire state. The high-class hotel also attracted several well-known celebrities over the years, including Gary

Cooper, Zane Grey, Bob Hope, John Wayne, Robert Englund, Anthony Hopkins, Michael J. Fox, and many others.

Although some hotels and tourist attractions would prefer to keep their hauntings under the radar, the Hotel Monte Vista embraces the fact that it is haunted. Their official website claims that at least ten separate ghosts have been identified and are known to haunt the hotel.

Perhaps the most infamous ghost that haunts the Hotel Monte Vista is that of a man who attempted to rob a Flagstaff bank in 1970. The story goes that in 1970, a group of three men successfully robbed a local bank. However, there was a shootout between the robbers and the bank guard during the robbery. One of the guard's bullets hit one of the three bank robbers as they fled. Thinking that the bullet had simply grazed him, the three men decided that medical attention could wait until after they reveled in the success of their robbery. The men went to the bar in the Hotel Monte Vista to have a few celebratory drinks.

During the second round of drinks, the injured man slumped over unconscious due to loss of blood. When he fell over, the injured man's companions noticed that he was bleeding profusely and a pool of blood soon formed on the floor beneath his bar stool. Realizing that their companion was either dead or was going to die shortly, the two men quietly finished their drinks and slipped out of the bar, knowing that the stolen money could now be divided into two, rather than three, equal parts. To the casual passerby, their dead friend looked just like another man who had one too many drinks. They left their newly deceased friend on the bar stool for the waitress to find.

There are those who believe that the bank robber's ghost still haunts the bar where he bled to death in 1970. People have seen a man sitting at a bar stool that is believed to be in the exact spot where the man died. Staff also claim to have noticed that bar stools and drinks have moved on their own accord. Ghost hunters who have investigated the area have allegedly recorded the EVP of a man's disembodied voice.

Several of the Hotel Monte Vista's rooms are reportedly haunted. Many rooms in the Monte Vista are named after the famous guests who were known to have stayed there. Two of the rooms, the Gary Cooper Room (room 306) and the Zane Grey Room (room 210) appear to be two of the most haunted rooms in the entire hotel.

Only a few blocks from the Hotel Monte Vista was the red-light district of Flagstaff in the early 1940s. Men were known to pick up prostitutes and take them to the hotel because of its overall appearance, cleanliness, and proximity to the red-light district. One night in the early 1940s, a man returned to the hotel with two women. As this was not an uncommon sight, the front-desk worker gave them a key to room 306 without a second thought. The three went to the room, and at some point in the night, the sound of a loud crash and breaking glass came from room 306 and awakened guests in the adjacent hotel rooms. When the guests looked out their windows, they saw that two women had either jumped or had been thrown out of the window of room 306 and their lifeless bodies lay on the concrete below. By the time authorities arrived on the scene of the double murder, the man who had rented the room had already fled. To this day, the crime has never been solved.

Since that day, guests who have stayed in room 306 often feel as if they are being watched while they are in their beds. Some people have even claimed to have the feeling of being watched accompanied by a tightness around their throat as if they were being choked. If this is the case, it may give a clue as to how these women may have died. A three-story fall would likely cause severe injuries such as broken bones, but a person could survive such a fall. For two people to die at the same time from such a height is not very likely. One theory is that the two women were strangled to death and then their dead bodies thrown out the window of room 306 to make it look like a double suicide.

Room 210 is known as the Zane Grey Room because the famous western author was known to check into the hotel in order to have an opportunity to write undisturbed. Over the years, people who have stayed in this room have heard a loud knock on their door in the middle of the night. When the guests check to see who is knocking and open the door, nobody is there and the hallway is empty. On rare occasions, the knock is accompanied by the sound of a young male voice that says, "Room service." Interestingly enough, when John Wayne stayed in this room, he claimed to have had experienced the ghost knocker, who has become known as the "phantom bellboy." When John Wayne told his story, he always added that he did not feel threatened by the experience and that the ghost seemed to be friendly.

Riordan Mansion State Park
1300 Riordan Ranch Street

The history of the Riordans in Arizona began with Dennis Riordan, who in 1884, came to Flagstaff from Chicago and became a manager at the Ayer Lumber Company. Seeing that business was good, he called for his two younger brothers, Timothy and Michael, to help. The business was so good that within a few years, Dennis Riordan purchased the company in 1887 and renamed it the Arizona Lumber and Timber Company. However, Dennis's wife, Celine, did not like the lifestyle associated with Flagstaff and eventually convinced Dennis to move back with her to Chicago. Timothy and Michael Riordan stayed in Flagstaff and took over the lumber business.

Becoming very wealthy from the profits of the Arizona Lumber and Timber Company, the Riordan brothers contributed considerably to the betterment of Flagstaff. They helped construct several area Catholic churches and schools. They were also responsible for the development and introduction of the Flagstaff Electric Company, which provided electricity for the first time to several members of the community.

Timothy and Michael Riordan met Elizabeth and Carolyn Metz, two sisters who lived in the area. Shortly after meeting, Timothy started to date Carolyn and Michael began to date Elizabeth. By 1889, the two couples had married. In 1904, the Riordan brothers began construction on a 13,000-square-foot mansion not far from downtown Flagstaff. The mansion was divided into three distinct sections. Two sections consisted of similar 6,000-square-foot living areas for each brother and their respective wives. These two sections were joined by a 1,000-square-foot common area that contained several rooms including a billiard room and a personal chapel. This common area became known as "the Cabin."

The chapel was very important to both of the Riordan families, as they were all very religious and attempted to attend church service in the town whenever possible. They constructed the chapel in the mansion's common area for when they were unable to attend service in town or simply wanted to take the time out to pray.

The Riordans had frequent visitors to their home, including members of the clergy, both local and traveling from out of town. Carolyn wanted to make an impression on her visitors and requested that a large statue of Jesus be placed in front of the chapel. She also arranged to have the statue illuminated at all times by electric light.

Rumor has it that while Carolyn was not at the mansion on April 24, 1943, staff at the mansion noticed that the lights that illuminated the Jesus statue in front of the chapel flickered and died. It was later determined that this electrical problem occurred at nearly the exact time that she died.

Some say that Carolyn is still at the Riordan mansion nearly seventy years after her death. Visitors and staff have reported seeing a woman standing near the Jesus statue at the chapel. Most believe this is the ghost of Carolyn.

Another haunting in the mansion's common area involves the Riorden brothers themselves. Timothy and Michael liked to play pool in the billiard room and were known to be found playing a game at all hours of the day or night. The sound of billiard balls hitting together can be heard on occasion in this room.

Comfi Cottages
1612 North Aztec

During the time that the Mother Road was extensively traveled in the 1930s through the 1960s, several different lodging options sprang up to suit the needs for people from all walks of life. A person could stay at a bed-and-breakfast, a four-star hotel that was frequented by celebrities, a campground, and even motel rooms that looked like teepees. However, few places actually offered a real "home away from home" feel like Comfi Cottages in Flagstaff.

Originally, all of the houses owned by Comfi Cottages were built as private residences. Since first opening, the owners of Comfi Cottages purchased several houses in the Flagstaff area and considerably renovated them with updated fixtures, appliances, and furniture. Today, there are nine separate houses owned by Comfi Cottages, each with its own personality. Each house has two to three bedrooms, a full kitchen, at least one full bath, a backyard with a fence, a fireplace, and all of the other amenities of home. It has everything that a family on vacation would want. One of the cottages even has its own resident ghost.

During the 1950s, the assistant postmaster of Flagstaff lived with his family at 919 North Beaver Street. He had a beautiful young daughter that he absolutely adored. Unfortunately, she contracted whooping cough and died in the house. The girl's father was devastated and soon moved out and placed the house up for sale. Although the house was in wonderful condition and in a nice neighborhood, not too many people were interested in purchasing it. The owners of Comfi Cottages found the house and since it was in a good neighborhood, decided to purchase it.

After some minor renovations, the house at 919 North Beaver Street was being used by guests and soon became one of Comfi Cottage's most popular houses. Shortly after the house was opened for guests, the owners started to hear stories from guests that led them to believe that it may be haunted by the eighteen-year-old daughter who died of whooping cough there in the 1950s.

Guests at the house have claimed to have felt a cool breeze in the room that was the girl's bedroom even though the window is closed and the air conditioner is turned off. Occasionally, guests in the bedroom have awakened to see a teenage girl standing by the window looking outside or standing beside the bed looking at them. A misty form has also been observed on the first floor by the staircase, although this has only been reported a few times. Because of the feelings of serenity associated with the girl's apparition, she has been nicknamed the "Teen Angel of Comfi Cottages."

After guests have reported the paranormal happenings at 919 North Beaver Street for years, the owners of Comfi Cottages received a visit from a man who claimed to be the girl's brother. He lived in the house when his sister died and decided to stop by his old home. He told the owners that his sister had in fact died in the second-floor bedroom where the ghostly activity took place. The girl's brother was kind enough to give the owners some black-and-white photographs of her. After he left, the owners kept photographs. When people who have seen the girl's apparition see the photographs, including family photos, they can always correctly identify the girl who died in that room.

Jerome

Jerome Grand Hotel
200 Hill Street

The building that would become known as the Jerome Grand Hotel was built in 1927, originally as the Jerome Verde Hospital. The hospital was built in part by contributions from the United Verde Mining Company because having a nearby hospital could mean the difference between life and death in the event of a cave-in or other mining accident. The hospital was built on Cleopatra Hill—the highest point in the entire Jerome area. At the time, the hospital was state of the art, provided more services, and able to take in more patients than any hospital within a fifty-mile area. The 30,000-square-foot Jerome Verde Hospital had five stories and had several hundred hospital beds.

Although the hospital offered services that other area medical facilities were not equipped to provide, it only stayed open twenty-three years. In the 1940s, the population of Jerome started to dwindle as people moved to areas that had better employment opportunities. Due to lack of work and a rapidly declining population, the Jerome Verde Hospital was forced to close its doors in 1950. The final mine in Jerome closed in 1953 and the population lowered even more to approximately fifty people. Today, there are about 400 people in Jerome.

The hospital remained closed for over forty years until it was purchased and renovated into its current incarnation as the Jerome Grand Hotel in 1996. As the original hospital was built to withstand dynamite blasts, it had a very solid foundation. Most of the renovations had more to do with wiring and plumbing than anything else. Although it was a major undertaking to turn the old hospital into a luxury hotel, the Jerome Grand Hotel has been very successful since opening. Many of the hospital rooms were converted into the hotel rooms and suites.

Unlike some places that try to shy away from their ghost stories, the official Jerome Grand Hotel website has a page dedicated to paranormal accounts. They even sponsor ghost hunts that take place on the property. There have been reports of ghosts haunting the hotel since shortly after it reopened in 1996. The stories that visitors have shared are extremely consistent with the stories that were told by staff and patients who were at the hospital before it closed.

Even before the Jerome Verde Hospital closed in 1950, it was no stranger to paranormal events. Several doctors, nurses, and patients all claimed to have had their own experiences with the supernatural. It did not affect the staff at the hospital because they had grown accustomed to the paranormal activity, but patients were sometimes baffled or frightened.

Most of the ghostly events at the Jerome Verde Hospital are simply the sounds of coughing, crying, or snippets of conversation coming from vacant rooms or in the empty hospital hallways and corridors. These have been recorded on many occasions as EVPs by ghost hunters who have investigated the hotel. Sometimes, hotel guests have heard the coughing and other sounds while in their room. In a few instances, they have found that the water in their room has turned on by itself or the lights to their room have either been turned on or off while they were sleeping.

One ghost that is known to haunt the Jerome Grand Hotel is that of hospital maintenance man Claude Harvey. One day in 1935, Harvey's body was found at the bottom of an elevator shaft. Apparently, he fell or was thrown into the elevator shaft and the weight of the elevator descended upon him and crushed him to death. Although it was written off as a freak accident, medical examiners determined that Harvey had a broken neck that was not consistent with a fall down the elevator shaft or with being crushed by the elevator itself. It was widely speculated for a few years that Claude Harvey had in fact been murdered and his body thrown down the shaft to make it look like an accident. However, there was no official investigation and nobody was arrested or even questioned. Over the years, the mysterious circumstances behind his death were forgotten.

After Claude Harvey's death, the power was shut off to the elevator and doors were sealed off to prevent it from being used again. Not long after this was done, employees and patients at the hospital have heard the sound of the elevator running and stopping at each of the floors. It has been said that the sound of the elevator can still be heard going from floor to floor to this day, even though it has not been in use since Claude Harvey's death.

The ghost that is most often experienced at the Grand Jerome Hotel is known simply as "the bearded man." Most people feel that the bearded man is the ghost of a former doctor at the hospital, although he has never been positively identified. He has been described as a tall man of medium build with a neatly trimmed beard. He is always described as wearing a white laboratory or physician's coat.

When he made his appearance, the bearded man would usually enter a patient's room to turn off their lights. When the nursing staff would check on the patient, they would ask why they turned out their light by the door. It should be noted that some of these patients were bedridden—too ill to get out of bed, walk to the light switch to turn it off, and return to their bed. Often, patients would ask their nurse who the nice, bearded doctor was. Depending on the patient, the nursing staff would inform the patient that there was nobody on staff that fit that description. The apparitions of the bearded man would only be seen on the second and third floors of the hospital, and has been occasionally seen by staff walking down the hallways or peeking into the doors to check on the patients.

Mile High Inn/Inn at Jerome
309 Main Street

The house that would become the Mile High Inn in 2004 was built as a private residence in 1899. Soon after it was built, the building developed a reputation for what took place behind the doors. During Jerome's busiest years as a mining community, this building was one of the busiest and most successful brothels for miles around. The business was owned by madame Jennie Banters. With a great business sense and the ability to provide what her customers wanted, Banters became one of the richest and most influential people in Jerome. However, one night, she was murdered by one of her customers who was drunk and had become violent against her.

The Mile High Inn is very active in regard to hauntings. There are at least four and as many as seven separate ghosts that have been identified at the Mile High Inn. The bed-and-breakfast has eight guest rooms. One of the three rooms that have paranormal activity has been called the Spooks, Ghost, and Goblin Room.

Jennie Banters's ghost has been seen and felt throughout the house after she was murdered, although she is most often experienced in the kitchen area. Jennie prided herself as being very neat and organized in all areas of her life. Perhaps the cleanliness and neat appearance of her brothel may have been influential in her success as a businesswoman and madame. She absolutely despised disarray and clutter. If Jennie's ghost finds that the kitchen area is in disarray and not well kept, such as leaving dirty dishes or food out, she will become very angry. Jennie's ghost has been known to express her anger at a cluttered kitchen by throwing and breaking dishes and glasses on the floor as well as opening the drawers and cabinet doors. It turns out that if the kitchen is kept clean on a daily basis, this poltergeist activity does not happen.

Jennie's ghost is not alone in the kitchen. Perhaps out of all the ghosts at the Mile High Inn, the most popular is Jennie's cat, who rarely left her side in life or, apparently, the afterlife. A light-colored cat has been seen dozens of times wandering throughout the first floor, particularly near the kitchen area. When people attempt to catch the cat, it will run into the kitchen where it has been known to disappear right before a person's eyes.

Although usually confined to the first floor, Jennie's cat has been seen sleeping on the bed in the room that was Jennie's when she was alive.

The cat is usually friendly, because people have been known to have her rub up against their legs. Also, the loud sound of purring can be heard on the first floor and in the bedroom where the cat's apparition has been seen.

There is also the ghost of a well-dressed older gentleman who has been seen in one of the bedrooms of the Mile High Inn. He is likely the ghost of one of the brothel's frequent customers. Usually, he can be sitting on the edge of a bed, pacing the floor, or standing in the doorway of one of the rooms.

Williams

....

Red Garter Inn

137 West Railroad Avenue

The Red Garter Inn at Williams was built in 1897 as a tavern and brothel for locals and visitors. It continued to function as a tavern and brothel well through the Prohibition era as a speakeasy up until the early 1940s, when it closed temporarily. In recent years, the Red Garter reopened as a bed-and-breakfast with three guest rooms known as the Madame's Room, the Honeymoon Suite, and the Parlor.

The Red Garter has had its share of drama over the years that may have contributed to it being haunted. One night a few years after the establishment opened, a prostitute had a disagreement with one of her customers. He was intoxicated and was becoming very belligerent and physically abusive toward her. She left the room and went into the hall in order to get away from him. He followed, and the fight continued in the hallway beside the staircase leading to the first floor. In self-defense, the woman pulled a knife and stabbed her assailant, who fell down the steps and staggered into the street, where he bled to death. No charges were filed as it was determined that she had been protecting herself.

Today, the man's ghost still haunts the Red Garter Inn. Sometimes the sounds of the argument can still be heard in the hallway on the second floor. Also, the hazy apparition of a large man can be seen at the top of the stairs and in the street in front of the building.

There are a few other ghosts that are said to haunt the Red Garter, including at least one prostitute whose apparition can be seen in one of the three guest rooms and the ghost of a man who has sometimes been seen on the first floor. Most likely, he was a customer at the brothel.

Oatman

·················

Oatman Hotel, Room 15

181 Main Street, Route 66

The Oatman hotel is a quiet two-story hotel that was built in downtown Oatman, Arizona, in 1921. At first glance, it does not appear that this hotel would be a likely place to be haunted. However, it has more than one active spirit inside.

In the late 1920s, an Irish immigrant named Charlie rented one of the rooms while he looked for work in the Oatman area. Like many immigrants, Charlie wanted to start a new life and hopefully make his fortune. However, things did not turn out as Charlie had hoped. Work was scarce and he desperately missed his native Ireland. He wanted to return home, but simply did not have the money to do so.

When he could afford it, Charlie stayed in room 15 of the Oatman Hotel. Through his longing to return to Ireland and his lack of stable employment, Charlie went into a depression and started to drink while at the hotel. He soon became a full-blown alcoholic. It was not uncommon to see Charlie intoxicated near or around the Oatman. Sometimes, he did not leave room 15 for a few days while he was drinking.

One night after a drinking bout, Charlie simply disappeared. Usually, he would greet the front-desk worker whenever he passed. However, the worker thought it was odd that Charlie was nowhere to be seen. Two days later, Charlie's body was found among some trash behind the Oatman Hotel. Penniless, Charlie could not afford a proper funeral or burial. His few belongings that were found in room 15 were gathered together and he was buried in a shallow, unmarked pauper's grave outside of town. As there was no marker, the actual location of Charlie's grave is no longer known.

Shortly after Charlie was buried, he started to make his presence known in room 15. Charlie had the peculiar habit of always sleeping with the window open. When guests stay in room 15 at the Oatman, they are usually surprised to find the window open in the middle of the night. They close the window only to find it open again a few minutes later. There is also the overwhelming feeling of being watched while in the room. On a few occasions, guests have seen shadowy forms in their peripheral vision.

New employees who did not know about Charlie simply call the ghost in room 15 "Oatie." Only after research was conducted and some of the older former employees were asked did the true identity of Charlie become known.

The Honeymoon Suite in the Oatman Hotel is also reported to be haunted. The room now known as the Honeymoon Suite is the room where famous movie star Clark Gable spent his wedding night. Today, people who have stayed in the Honeymoon Suite believe that it is haunted by the ghost of a man who fits Clark Gable's description. He is usually seen walking back and forth in the room for a few seconds before he disappears.

Another haunted location in the Oatman Hotel is the bar area. Although there have not been any stories told, it would not be surprising if Charlie's ghost was seen at the bar. Instead, in this area the sound of a few men playing poker can be heard late at night even if the bar is empty.

Lake Havasu City

London Bridge

London Bridge was originally built in 1824 for pedestrians and traffic to cross the Thames River in London, England. The bridge became so necessary to London life that during its busiest times, as many as 8,000 people and 900 vehicles crossed it every hour. After more than one hundred years of use, it was noticed that London Bridge was in danger of collapsing after it had sank several inches due to constant heavy traffic.

Rather than simply demolishing London Bridge, the decision was made to sell it at an auction. The auction took place in 1967, and an American by the name of Robert McCullough won the auction by paying an estimated $2,460,000 for the bridge. If most Englishmen thought that an American purchasing London Bridge was an absurd idea, then what McCullough decided to do next was absolutely insane.

McCullough arranged to have London Bridge taken apart brick by brick. He made certain that each individual brick was numbered and marked so that it could be reassembled in its proper order when he put it back together in Lake Havasu, Arizona. The entire process of dismantling London Bridge, shipping the bricks to Arizona, and reconstructing it took approximately four years to complete.

Once it was completed, McCullough opened London Bridge as a tourist attraction that included several authentic items from London, including a double-decker bus and a red telephone box. He also added other English-themed tourist attractions under the bridge, including an English shopping center that sold a variety of English goods and souvenirs. Within a few years, London Bridge at Lake Havasu had become Arizona's largest tourist attraction aside from the Grand Canyon.

When McCullough brought London Bridge to Arizona, it appears that he also happened to bring some authentic English ghosts with it as well.

As it took from 1967 to 1971 for McCullough to completely rebuild London Bridge at Lake Havasu, the official dedication of the bridge took place on October 10, 1971. That also so happens to be the date the people started to notice the ghosts of London Bridge.

During the dedication ceremony, a woman noticed four people wearing 1800s clothing crossing London Bridge. As the dedication was underway, the bridge should have been clear of pedestrians. The woman pointed the four people out to some other bystanders, who thought that they must be dressed in period clothing in order to entertain the crowds after the dedication ceremony. When the four people were about halfway across London

Bridge, they suddenly vanished. Although this is the first documented case of London Bridge being haunted, it certainly would not be the last. In the years since it opened, hundreds of tourists have reported seeing the same four people walking across London Bridge only to watch them disappear about halfway across the structure.

There are other ghosts that have been associated with Lake Havasu's London Bridge. Occasionally, when people cross the bridge, they get an overwhelming sensation that several people are bustling past them. Some people have even claimed to have been bumped into by some unseen pedestrian.

Another ghost that has commonly been connected to the Lake Havasu London Bridge is that of a uniformed police officer, or bobby, as they are referred to in England. The police officer's apparition appears to be patrolling the bridge.

EIGHT

CALIFORNIA

314 miles

California's Santa Monica Pier marks the official end point of Route 66, but there are several great sights to take in and ghost stories to hear along the final 314 miles of the Mother Road. Many ghost stories from California illustrate the extremes of the human experience. They take us from the shadows of abandoned ghost towns to the elaborate grounds of one-of-a-kind mansions and from secluded bungalows to a location where hundreds of people have taken their lives in public.

California has been the home to outspoken and wonderful celebrities for well over a century. Some famous stars are so devoted to their fans that an inconvenience such as death won't keep them from making an appearance from time

to time. There are many places in California that tourists actually seek out in hopes of trying to get a personal ghostly encounter of a departed celebrity and in many cases they are not disappointed. As they say in show biz, the show must go on …

Needles

Sam Kinison

US Route 95

Actor and comedian Sam Kinison was killed in an automobile accident near Needles, California, on April 10, 1992. He and his newlywed wife were only married five days before the accident happened on US Route 95, near I-40. He was struck head-on by a seventeen-year-old boy driving a pickup truck. Although Kinison's wife survived the accident, Kinison was killed, and the 1989 Trans Am that he was driving was completely destroyed. People say that on certain nights at the accident site, you can see Kinison's white Trans Am appear for a few seconds, then suddenly disappear. Occasionally, the sounds of screeching brakes and crashing metal can also be heard.

Newberry Springs

Minnolea Road

This is likely a variation of the Llorona legend (the weeping woman) that has been told and retold in several communities in the western states. However, it does warrant sharing if for nothing else than to illustrate the difference between legends and actual accounts of the paranormal. Generally, legends tend to be more vague and are usually told by third- or fourth-hand observations … a friend of a friend of a friend told me about this place that is haunted. An actual haunting is usually experienced by people firsthand. With a legend, there does not appear to be any written documentation of an event that may have led to it coming into being.

With a haunting, often there are newspaper stories, obituaries, or other documentation that can at the very least give some credence to an event that actually happened.

That being said, there is a legend of a "hatchet lady" who can be seen in a dry river bottom between Minnolea and Harvard Roads in Newberry Springs. Accounts vary as to who this woman actually was when she was alive. Some people believe that she was a settler's wife who was caught off guard in the riverbed and accidently drowned. Another version states that the Hatchet Lady found her husband with another woman and beheaded him with a hatchet before killing herself. No matter which version you believe, there have been reports from people living nearby to have seen a woman in clothing from the 1800s carrying a bloody hatchet in the river-bed during the dry months that the desert is famous for.

Calico

Calico Ghost Town

Calico, California, had its humble beginnings back in 1881 when four men went prospecting for silver in a mountain range of what is now known as the Calico Mountains. They found one of the largest veins of silver in California up until that time. Soon, the town of Calico was built near where the mines were located. By 1885, the town had a population of over 1,100, several businesses including three hotels, a post office, a newspaper, and a school. Calico was definitely a boom town that sprang up literally almost overnight.

However, less than fifteen years after the four men found silver, Calico's luck had changed for the worse, mainly due to the price of silver bottoming out to less than $0.60 per troy ounce in 1897. The post office, school, hotels, and most of the other businesses in Calico had closed. All but a few of the most loyal residents moved away and Calico became a ghost town almost as quickly as it had been placed on the map in 1881.

In the 1950s, there was an attempt to restore as much of the town to its former condition and in 1962, Calico was designated a historical landmark. Only a few of the buildings from Calico were still standing at that time, so a great deal of time, material, and money were invested into making Calico into a mining town that visitors could experience.

Today, Calico is a popular tourist attraction and has been given the title of Official State Silver Rush Ghost Town. Thousands of tourists from all over the country come to visit the Calico Ghost Town every year. Staged gunfights and other performances take place in downtown Calico every day. Kids can experience what it was like to pan for gold and other precious metals just like the prospectors did over one hundred twenty-five years ago. It has a museum that allows visitors to look at items that were actually used before Calico became a ghost town.

Although Calico is a living testament to the gold and silver rush of the late 1800s, there is a side to Calico that not many visitors to the town may be aware of. Many of the original buildings that are still standing and many of the mines in the hills surrounding Calico are haunted by the people who once lived here.

Two of those buildings are the Lane Home Needlepoint store and Lil's Saloon.

Lane Home Needlepoint Store

The Lane Home Needlepoint store is one of the few original structures in Calico today. Originally, this attraction was the private home of Lucy Lane, longtime resident of Calico. Today, the home is used as a store and museum. One of Lucy Lane's favorite pieces of furniture currently on display was her old wicker rocking chair. Lucy was known to sit back in her rocking chair for hours at a time. An inconvenience such as death was not enough for Lucy to stop rocking. Visitors and staff working at the needlepoint store have seen Lucy's empty rocking chair start to move lightly back and forth on its own accord when nobody is near it.

An apparition of a woman believed to be Lucy Lane has been seen walking from the needlepoint store toward the location where the general store once stood in town. The apparition always seems to disappear just at the front of the general store.

Pictures and other wall hangings for sale in the needlepoint store have also been placed in neat piles on the floor in the center of the rooms on occasion after the store is closed for the night. It is believed that Lucy may not realize that she is deceased and may be trying to put things back to the way they were when she was alive.

Lil's Saloon

Another original building from Calico's past that is haunted is Lil's Saloon. Of the three saloons in Calico, Lil's was considered by some to be the most popular. Although there was the occasional fight at Lil's, problems rarely got out of hand. It was the place for a miner or prospector to relax after a long week of searching for precious metals or the first place to go to celebrate once they found a fortune.

Although there are not many apparitions associated with Lil's Saloon, that does not mean that it is not haunted. People visiting Lil's over the past several years have heard the loud sounds of partying crowds coming from within the empty saloon. The sounds of loud singing and piano playing have also been heard from people walking on the streets outside of Lil's Saloon.

Old Schoolhouse

The old schoolhouse is located on top of a hill overlooking the town. Although the old schoolhouse is not one of the original buildings left in Calico, a replica was reconstructed on the exact spot of the original schoolhouse. When the replica was rebuilt, every effort was made to create a duplicate of the old schoolhouse. There are two or three ghosts associated with the old schoolhouse that can be seen there today.

Visitors to the Calico Ghost Town have seen a girl about ten years old peeking out of one of the schoolhouse's dusty windows. A lone child between six and eight years old can also be seen playing in the area around the schoolhouse. By the time concerned people reach the schoolhouse to try to help the children find their parents, there are no signs that the children were ever there at all.

In addition to the two children, the old schoolhouse appears to be haunted by a woman wearing a long dress. She is seen at the school's front entrance and appears as if she is calling children into the school from recess. It is believed that this apparition is of the schoolteacher that was in Calico during the town's more prosperous days.

The Calico Mines

The mines that were responsible for both Calico's creation and ultimate downfall are located in the hills and mountains that surround the little ghost town. There are several dozen mines scattered through the mountains, some of which have not been seen by humans in over one hundred years. There are about 1,000 feet of mines near Calico that have been made safe enough for visitors to tour so that they can get a full experience of what it is like to work in a mine.

It was not unheard of for people to die on a fairly regular basis in Calico by a mine collapse or similar accident. As a result, many of the mines behind Calico are said to be haunted. At one mine, people have seen a man with a pickax resting on his shoulder standing at the mouth of the mineshaft. Another mine that was owned by two brothers named Mulchaey is supposedly haunted by one or both of the brothers. The Mulchaey brothers actually lived in their mine for a time in order to protect their investment and to save money that would normally have been spent on lodging in Calico. Although most of this mine is closed to the public, one section of the Mulchaey mine can be toured by the public. On some tours, people have heard two people with accented voices in conversation in an area that is off limits to tourists for safety reasons. It is believed that the voices are actually those of the Mulchaey brothers, who were once so protective of and dedicated to their mine.

Although Lil's Saloon, the Lane Home Needlepont store, the Old Schoolhouse, and the mines outside of town seem to be where most of the hauntngs occur, one could argue that the entire town of Calico is haunted. There are two individual hauntings that are not necessarily associated with any one building in Calico. These two individuals became legends in Calico when they were alive, and it is safe to reason that they are continuing to create a name for themselves long after they have died. These two ghosts are of Tumbleweed Harris and Dorsey the Dog.

Tumbleweed Harris

It has been said by all who knew him that one of the town's most popular constables, Tumbleweed Harris, had always been dedicated to keeping the town of Calico safe. Although Tumbleweed Harris died in the 1970s, he is still seen walking down the main street of Calico on a regular basis. Witnesses who have seen his ghost describe Tumbleweed Harris as a formidable, broad-shouldered man with a white beard and a large cowboy hat. He is usually seen walking down the main boardwalk of Calico, not far from where the sheriff's office was originally located. If you want to visit Tumbleweed Harris's gravesite, he is buried in a grave on a hill overlooking Calico today.

Dorsey the Dog

Not all of the ghosts in Calico are human. One of the most famous residents in the 1880s was Dorsey, the mail-carrying dog. In Kenny Rogers's 1972 album *The Ballad of Calico*, an entire song is dedicated to Dorsey. The black-and-white shepherd mix was found by postmaster Jim Stacy abandoned in front of the post office in 1883. The postmaster named him Dorsey, and he soon became a fixture at the Calico post office. A few months after the postmaster took him in, Dorsey's hidden talent was revealed.

The postmaster needed to send a message to the miner a few miles away in Bismarck, so he tied a note to Dorsey's back and sent him to find the man. The postmaster was surprised to see Dorsey return soon with a reply from the miner. Within a short time, Dorsey was carrying the mail from Calico to Bismarck on a regular basis. Dorsey was outfitted with a small backpack to carry letters back and forth, and he did so for about three years.

Today, a small shadowy apparition about the size of a dog has been seen several times near where the original Calico post office once stood. If approached, the shadowy form will run in the direction of the mines in Bismarck. Sometimes, barking can be heard accompanying the shadow when it is seen. There is little doubt that this is actually the ghost of Dorsey, the Mail-Carrying Dog.

Barstow

Casa del Desierto/Harvey House Railroad Depot
685 North First Street

The Casa del Desierto (House of the Desert) was a train depot and hotel built in 1911 to accommodate railroad passengers visiting or passing through Barstow after the old train station burned to the ground in 1908. Casa del Desierto was designed by the Fred Harvey Company, which built nearly ninety Harvey Houses at train stations throughout the United States. Harvey House was the first restaurant chain in the United States, and provided quality meals to people traveling via railway.

The waitresses who worked at Harvey Houses were known as Harvey Girls. They were generally young, attractive women between eighteen and twenty-five years old. Since most women who applied were turned down, it was truly an honor to be hired as a Harvey Girl. In 1942, Samuel Hopkins Adams wrote a novel called *The Harvey Girls*, which was adapted into a 1946 movie by the same name starring Angela Lansbury and Judy Garland.

Every Harvey Girl had to follow a series of very strict guidelines in order to be employed, including abiding by a 10:00 p.m. curfew every night. Being out after 10:00 p.m. was considered grounds for termination because the Harvey Houses needed all of their waitresses to be well rested for work the following day. Working as a Harvey Girl also consisted of wearing the traditional Harvey Girl uniform, which was a very conservative black-and-white uniform that had to be pressed prior to each shift.

In the early to mid-1950s, more people started to drive or fly to their destinations, which meant that fewer people opted to travel by railroad. Due to this, most Harvey Houses closed during this time, including the Casa del Desierto, which closed down in 1959. Today, the Casa del Desierto is used to house the Western America Railroad Museum and the Barstow Route 66 Museum.

In regard to hauntings, the Casa del Desierto is haunted by the ghost of a Harvey Girl named Rachel, who worked there in the 1920s. Rachel can be seen in her traditional black-and-white uniform near where the dining area of the Casa del Desietro was once located. She appears to be taking orders for customers in much the same manner that she would have done when she was alive.

Devore

Oakdale Guest Ranch/Treehouse Fun Ranch
17809 Glen Helen

Apparently, Treehouse Fun Ranch is haunted by a truck driver who frequented the nudist colony when he was alive, and loved the place so much that he had arranged to have a friend bring his ashes there after he died. The friend took the urn containing his friend's ashes to a bar that was on the property. It is uncertain what happened next, but the bartender obtained the ashes and placed them behind the bar where they were forgotten by everybody. Years later, the Treehouse was sold. The new owners were renovating the buildings on the grounds and when the bar was cleaned, the truck driver's urn was found. After the ashes were moved, poltergeist activity started to take place at the Treehouse Fun Ranch. Guests and workers have reported that the fire pit on site will light itself. Also, there are electrical disturbances with lights, small appliances, and battery-operated devices such as flashlights and cameras that are typical of hauntings.

San Bernardino

California Theatre of the Performing Arts
562 West 4th Street

The California Theatre for Performing Arts opened in 1928 and has operated continuously ever since. During the 1930s, several movie studios would often premiere their films at the California Theatre before their national release. Often, the stars of these movies and other celebrities would show up at these premieres.

The 1,718-seat theater has hosted several types of entertainment over the years. It has been a vaudeville theater, a movie theater, and concert hall that has hosted some of the greatest performers of our time, such as Clark Gable, Yul Brynner, Penn and Teller, Tom Arnold, and Will Rogers.

In August 1935, movie star and political satirist Will Rogers gave his final public performance at the California Theatre. A few days after leaving the California Theatre, on August 15, 1935, Will Rogers was flying from Fairbanks, Alaska, to Point Barrow, Alaska, with friend and aviator Wiley Post in a Lockheed Orion-Explorer. A few miles from Point Barrow, Post landed their plane in order to ask for directions because he felt that they were lost. After taking off again, the plane stalled and crashed upside down in a body of water, killing both Post and Rogers instantly.

After the plane crash that led to Will Rogers's death, performers and other people backstage have seen his apparition in the dressing room that he used for his August 1935 performance. Although he is not seen as often today, people still claim to see Will Rogers's ghost in the dressing room preparing to go on stage for his final performance.

Aqua Mausa Cemetery
2001 West Agua Mausa Road
The Aqua Mausa cemetery is an old, nearly abandoned cemetery located on an out-of-the-way road a few miles from downtown San Bernandino.

Several years ago, two people were found shot execution style along the road not far from the cemetery. Although an investigation was conducted to try to identify the killer, the crime was never solved. It has been said that if a person walks near the cemetery, he or she can sometimes hear two loud gunshots coming from the area the victims' bodies were discovered.

A second haunting experienced near the old cemetery occurs much more frequently. The apparition of an old man walking his dog has been known to appear on the road near the cemetery. The old man's ghost will sometimes appear so suddenly that drivers will often slam on their brakes or swerve in order to miss them. A few times, a driver can feel a distinct thud as if they hit a pedestrian. When the person gets out of their car to check on the old man, the road is always empty.

It is believed that either an unidentified man was walking his dog on Aqua Mausa Road when they were struck along the street near the cemetery or that the apparition is the ghost of a man who was buried in the cemetery.

Rancho Cucamonga

The Sycamore Inn
8318 Foothill Boulevard
The original Sycamore Inn was built in 1848 as a stop for travelers using the Butterfield Stagecoach Line. When it was opened, proprietor William "Uncle Billy" Rubottom called it the Mountain View Inn. The Mountain

View Inn offered a choice of eight comfortable rooms, hot baths, a full restaurant, and several other amenities that the weary stagecoach traveler would pay top dollar for.

Rubottom was originally from Missouri and had moved to the Rancho Cucamonga area shortly before opening the Mountain View Inn. He provided traditional Southern hospitality for all his guests and neighbors and soon had regulars that came to the Mountain View Inn just as much for the atmosphere as anything else. His restaurant served traditional Southern cuisine such as fried chicken, biscuits, grits, and the like, which soon became a favorite in the area. Rubottom was making quite a nice living for himself in Rancho Cucamonga.

Despite his Southern charm, Rubottom had a past—there was a definite reason why he moved to California from Missouri. According to some accounts, before opening the Mountain View Inn, Rubottom had killed two men in Arkansas. Soon, other rumors started to come to the surface about Rubottom, including suspicion that he shot and killed his own son-in-law just before moving to California.

Often, our past mistakes and actions can come back to haunt us. That certainly seems to be the case with Rubottom. While he was proprietor, at least two murders took place at the Mountain View Inn. In 1862, local resident and regular patron John Rains was murdered in the restaurant's dining area after a heated argument led to a physical altercation between him and another man. The argument likely had something to do with Rains's wife, Maria.

That evening, before going to the restaurant, Rains's wife had hidden his guns, leaving him unarmed and unable to protect himself from his assailant. Not long after John Rains was buried, word got out that Maria had planned the entire incident beforehand. This infuriated several residents, and soon a posse of at least ten men went searching for Maria Rains and caught up to her at Rubottom's establishment, the Mountain View Inn. Rubottom realized the men meant to harm her, and he made them all remove their firearms before he would allow them to enter. They looked throughout the inn, but were unable to find her. It is possible that Rubottom was hiding her.

Two years later, in 1864, Maria Rains was in a carriage with her dead husband's ranch manager, Ramón Carillo. It was believed that the two were lovers before John Rains died, which may have been a motive for his murder. An unknown man approached the carriage and shot Carillo at close range, fatally wounding him. Carillo was able to crawl to the steps of the Mountain View Inn, where he died of his gunshot wound.

The Mountain View Inn was still a very popular destination for travelers until it burned down in the early 1900s. It was rebuilt in 1920 on the same spot. In 1939, the Mountain View Inn was sold and the name was changed to the Sycamore Inn. Several updates and renovations were made to the inn to accommodate travelers. The guest rooms were closed off and the establishment focused exclusively on providing good food at a good price to people traveling through Rancho Cucamonga.

During Route 66's heyday, the Sycamore Inn had become a legend for people traveling the Mother Road. The Sycamore Inn became so popular from the 1930s to the 1960s that some famous celebrities would be seen here to get away from the fast-paced Hollywood lifestyle. There are some accounts that Marilyn Monroe and even Elizabeth Short (the Black Dahlia) were known to have visited the Sycamore Inn shortly before their respective deaths.

For years after it was rebuilt in 1920, patrons and employees alike have believed that the Sycamore Inn is haunted by at least one ghost from its earlier days as the Mountain View Inn. There are times that the solid apparition of a man in his mid-to-late twenties wearing a cowboy hat, jeans, and a duster can be seen walking in front of the restaurant before he suddenly disappears at the door. Some believe that this is the ghost of Ramón Carillo, who died at the doorsteps of the Mountain View Inn in 1864.

Pomona

....

Spadra Cemetery

2850 Pomona Boulevard

Spadra was a small community that sprang up because of the growing number of stagecoach lines that were forming in the 1860s in this part of California. Ironically, the town was named in 1866 by William Rubottom, the owner of the Mountain View Inn.

Due to the frequent stops made by stagecoaches from the Butterfield Stagecoach Line, Spadra soon began to grow considerably. Within a year after being established, Spadra had its own post office (one of the first ten post offices in the entire state of California), a schoolhouse, and several other businesses.

Although it had a promising future, a few years after Spadra became a town, another nearby settlement by the name of Pomona was established. Within a few years, Pomona overtook and replaced Spadra, which eventually became a ghost town. Eventually, Pomona grew to the point that it had absorbed the few buildings that were left of Spadra. Today, the only namesake for the town of Spadra is the Spadra Cemetery, located on Pomona Boulevard.

Originally named the Old Settlers' Cemetery, the name was changed to Spadra Cemetery shortly after the post office was established in 1868. There are 212 graves in Spadra Cemetery, and the most recent burial was in 1955. Over the last ten to fifteen years, the cemetery went into disrepair and local gangs had defaced, destroyed, or stolen many of the original tombstones. Because of the excessive vandalism of the gravestones, the cemetery was closed to the public in the 1990s.

One ghost that is believed to haunt the Spadra Cemetery was a man by the name of Lee Warner.

Pearl Scott Hopp was in her early twenties when she married a wealthy, thirty-something store owner in Spadra. Soon after she married, Pearl had an affair with a local resident named Lee Warner. One night in 1909, Pearl had a very loud and violent argument near her father's home. Neighbors heard the argument, two gunshots, and then silence. They went to check on Pearl and found both her and Lee Warner dead. It was apparent that Lee had first killed Pearl and then turned the gun on himself. Both were buried in the Spadra Cemetery.

After they were buried, people started to see a woman carrying a small child through the cemetery, walking toward the same gravesite each time she is seen. Investigators believe that the gravesite belongs to Pearl Hopp. A second ghost is of a man who is seen wandering the graveyard as if he is looking for something. It is believed that this is the ghost of Lee Warner, who is constantly looking for Pearl Hopp.

Pasadena
·····················

Colorado Street Bridge/Suicide Bridge
Colorado Street

HAER No. CA-58-5

The Colorado Bridge (image courtesy Library of Congress)

The 1,467-foot Colorado Street Bridge in Pasadena was constructed in 1913 to cross the Arroyo Seco River. The size and beauty of the Colorado Street Bridge have brought people to see it on a daily basis for years. People who traveled Route 66 would sometimes cross it on the final stretch of the journey to the Santa Monica Pier, the official end of the Mother Road.

However, the 150-foot drop to the Arroyo Seco below has attracted an entirely unexpected and unwelcome kind of visitor to the Colorado Street Bridge. Within a few years after its construction, it was discovered that people were jumping from the bridge to their deaths on a fairly regular basis. The first documented jumper from the Colorado Street Bridge occurred in November 1919, but there were undoubtedly several suicides that were not documented that occurred prior to that date.

By 1923, so many people had jumped to their deaths from the Colorado Street Bridge that it became known as Suicide Bridge. Over the years, between one hundred and two hundred individuals have jumped to their deaths from Suicide Bridge.

People who have walked across the bridge will sometimes describe an overwhelming sense of depression and hopelessness, which may be residual energy left behind by the number of people who have died here.

There have been a few stories of hauntings associated with Suicide Bridge. One story is of a construction worker who died while pouring concrete while the Colorado Street Bridge was being built. The worker reportedly slipped and fell into the concrete he was working with. By the time his coworkers found out what happened, the concrete had mostly hardened. Rather than attempt to retrieve his body, it was decided that the bridge should be his final resting place and construction continued around his body. Sometimes, people have seen a man working on the bridge who will disappear after a few seconds.

Another ghost story associated with Suicide Bridge is that of a man who has been seen climbing up the side of the bridge and jumping off. The man has been described as wearing clothing that was in style in the 1930s, so it is likely that the ghost is of a man who committed suicide from the bridge sometime during the Great Depression.

Devils Gate Reservoir

The Devil's Gate Reservoir (image courtesy Library of Congress)

John Whiteside Parsons was a wealthy, charismatic, and brilliant rocket scientist in the 1940s who was one of the founders of the Jet Propulsion Laboratories, which has been instrumental to establishing today's American space program.

Although most of his colleagues felt that he was a technological genius, Parsons had a darker, secret life that fewer people were aware of. Parsons was obsessed with the occult and was actually a disciple of Aleister Crowley. Parsons often hosted elaborate ceremonies at his Pasadena mansion. One of his frequent guests to the ceremonies was L. Ron Hubbard, science-fiction author and founder of Scientology.

Aleister Crowley had commented on more than one occasion that he believed the area now known as the Devils' Gate Reservoir could contain an opening to another dimension. Parsons was so impressed with what Crowley had said that he used his charismatic influence to arrange to have the Jet Propulsion Laboratories built within a mile of Devil's Gate Reservoir in hopes that its mystical power could somehow influence the laboratory's success.

In the 1940s, Parsons continued to study Crowley and took an interest in performing several sex magick rituals at his mansion. His plan was that, through the rituals, he would help to arrange the conception of a "moon child." The moon child would theoretically take over the world as we knew it and open up a whole new age of power, magick, and enlightenment. A rocket scientist by day and a high-ranking occultist by night, John Parsons was a very ambitious man indeed.

According to some people who were present at the ceremonies Parsons hosted at his mansion, he did not succeed in bringing forth a moon child into the world, but rather he accidently opened up a portal between our dimension and another, much darker world. The portal was allegedly centered near a natural rock formation that looks like a devil's face, hence the origin of the name Devil's Gate.

According to Native American legend, for hundreds of years before Europeans settled this area, it was considered cursed and was avoided by the tribes. It is possible that the Native Americans could pick up that the veil between this dimension and another was thin at Devil's Gate, and therefore they wanted nothing to do with it. Apparently, Parsons was interested in the Devil's Gate area for the same reason.

There have been at least six disappearances at the reservoir since John Parsons allegedly performed his ceremonies. Two of the six disappearances can be traced to serial killer Mack Ray Edwards, who admitted to kidnapping and killing two boys on August 5, 1956. Edwards claimed he was not responsible for the other four disappearances, which remain unsolved to this day.

Rumors were even going around that Parsons himself could have been responsible for their disappearances, although there was never any evidence and he was never considered a suspect.

In addition to the disappearances, people who have camped nearby have claimed to hear strange screeches and howls outside of their tents. The sounds are sometimes accompanied by a bright, eerie glow that illuminates the entire area for a few seconds.

Los Angeles

....

Oban Hotel

6364 Yucca Street

The Oban Hotel was built in 1927 as a hotel for the everyday person. While most hotels in the Los Angeles area were designed for the powerful and wealthy, the Oban Hotel catered to those visiting Hollywood on a budget or actors just starting out in the movies, hoping to make it big one day. Several notable people stayed at the Oban when they were first starting out. Famous people associated with the Oban include James Dean, Clark Gable, Marilyn Monroe, and Orson Welles. The Oban Hotel recently went through several renovations and is now known as the Hollywood Hotel.

There are two ghosts that haunt the Oban Hotel. The first ghost has been identified as stuntman Charles Love, who shot himself while staying in room 311 or 312 on February 18, 1933. Since his suicide, guests in both of these rooms have reported seeing the apparition of a man standing near the bed. They have also reported that the temperature in the rooms suddenly gets several degrees colder, although the heating units are working properly. Other people have reported that they can hear people walking and talking loudly in the hallway right outside their room. When they open the door, the hallway is always empty.

Another ghost that haunts the Oban Hotel is that of a woman who is seen in the lobby wearing a white dress or uniform. Although she is not encountered as often as Love's ghost, several people have seen her and described her to the Oban Hotel staff. It is believed that she is the ghost of a cleaning lady or maid who worked at the hotel in the 1930s.

Ambassador Hotel
7617 S Figueroa Street

The Ambassador Hotel was opened for business on January 1, 1921. This lavish hotel soon gained a reputation as a magnet for movie stars, musicians, and politicians. The Ambassador Hotel was used to host six Academy Award Ceremonies from 1930 to 1943. Seven U.S. presidents have been reported to stay at the hotel while visiting California. In 1944, the first annual Golden Globes Awards Ceremony was held at the Ambassador Hotel's ballroom.

The Cocoanut Grove nightclub that was connected to the Ambassador Hotel brought such venues as Frank Sinatra, Nat King Cole, Dizzy Gillespie, Little Richard, and Natalie Cole. To say that the Ambassador Hotel and the Cocoanut Grove nightclub was the crème de la crème of hotels would be an understatement. It was *the* place to be if you wanted to rub elbows with the world's most well-known and powerful personalities.

On June 5, 1968, politician Robert F. Kennedy was shot in the Embassy Ballroom of the Ambassador Hotel. He had just won the California Democratic primary election and was celebrating his victory when Sirhan Sirhan shot Kennedy and five other people in the ballroom. Kennedy was rushed to a local hospital, where he died the next day. After Kennedy's assassination, people started to avoid the hotel, and eventually it closed its doors in 1989, although some movies and television shows were filmed there until 2004.

Regarding ghosts and paranormal activity experienced at the Ambassador Hotel, there have been several sightings over the years. The most notable is that, after Kennedy's assassination in 1968, people who went to the Embassy Ballroom were often overcome by a very strong sense of sadness and despair. In addition, there is a cold spot in the area where Kennedy and five other people were shot. Furthermore, after 1968, the hotel began to experience unexplained electrical problems in the ballroom and the nightclub. There were no known apparitions reported of Kennedy at the Ambassador Hotel.

Another ghost is that of a woman who was sometimes seen on the balcony of one of the fourth-floor rooms. She appeared to be wearing either a light-colored dress or a nightgown. People who have seen this woman's apparition all say that she appeared to be leaning over the edge of the balcony and started to fall over. At that point, the apparition simply disappeared. It has been speculated that either the woman seen falling had too much to drink and accidently fell over the balcony or that she jumped.

During its long life, several movies were filmed at the Ambassador Hotel. Some of the more notable films that used the Ambassador Hotel include *The Graduate, Pretty Woman, Forrest Gump, Catch Me If You Can,* and *Fear and Loathing in Las Vegas.*

On January 16, 2006, final demolition of the Ambassador Hotel was completed. The hotel was such a fixture in the Los Angeles community that a wake attended by hundreds of people was held on February 2, 2006, at the site where the Ambassador used to stand. Today, the site is home to two children's learning centers and the Robert F. Kennedy Memorial Park.

One question remains about the Ambassador. Is the area where it once stood still haunted? Although paranormal activity has decreased since the Ambassador Hotel was demolished in 2006, some people who go to the Robert F. Kennedy Memorial Park claim to feel a presence that intently watches them.

Biltmore Hotel/ Black Dahlia
506 South Grand Avenue

When the Biltmore Hotel was built in 1922 and opened in 1923, it was the largest hotel west of the Mississippi River, measuring over 70,000 square feet and boasting 1,500 guest rooms.

The Biltmore Hotel was one of the last places that Elizabeth Short was seen alive on January 8, 1947. Seven days later, on January 15, 1947, Elizabeth Short's mutilated body was found in a vacant lot on South Norton Avenue by a young mother walking with her three-year-old daughter. The mother immediately called police, who were quick to investigate.

According to autopsy reports and police files, Short's nude and muti-lated body had been neatly sliced in half at the waist. In addition, her body was completely bled dry. Her face was severely disfigured with what is known as a Glasgow Smile. This is when the corners of the mouth are cut through the cheek and up toward the ears. People who survive this ordeal have very prominent scars that give the impression of a very wide, hideous smile. Finally, Short's body had been washed and cleaned. Her upper body was posed with both arms outstretched above her head with her elbows forming right angles. Needless to say, there is little doubt that Elizabeth Short suffered horribly before she died.

Word soon got out about Short's murder and speculation soon turned into pure fabrication by the reporters covering the story. Some reporters were more interested in newspaper sales rather than accurately providing details about Short's murder. Bevo Means, a reporter for the *Los Angeles Herald Examiner* was first used the words "Black Dahlia" to describe Eliza-beth Short. The name stuck and people have known Elizabeth Short as "the Black Dahlia" ever since. To this day, Elizabeth Short's murder has yet to be solved.

After the story of the murder eventually died down, life returned to normal for most people. This is when guests at the Biltmore Hotel noticed a woman dressed in black fitting the description of Elizabeth Short pac-ing in the main lobby where the telephones used to be located in 1947. The apparition is usually silent and will disappear when approached. Other people have seen a similar ghost either walking toward the eleva-tors or leaving the hotel through the main entrance. People encounter this apparition even to this day.

Employees at the Biltmore have also claimed that there is something strange about the tenth floor. In the VIP lounge and some nearby suites on the tenth floor, there is an oppressive feeling of uneasiness and sorrow. Sometimes, when the staff prepare the rooms for the next guest and are positive they have changed the sheets and made the beds, they will sometimes return to find the beds unmade.

Finally, we cannot forget that the Biltmore Hotel was featured in the original *Ghostbusters* movie. The scene where the first ghost was captured with the proton packs by the Ghostbusters in the Sedgewick Hotel was actually filmed on location at the Biltmore Hotel. Whether the crew for the movie actually experienced the ghost of Elizabeth Short or of any other ghosts in the elaborate Biltmore Hotel is uncertain.

Building 26, Venice Beach Boardwalk
Westminster Avenue

Silent film star Charlie Chaplin had a particular affinity for the Venice Beach Boardwalk. During the height of his movie career, he made certain that several were filmed on or near the boardwalk. He owned several of the buildings, many of which were used as vacation spots by the wealthy.

However, there is one mystery that surrounds Charlie Chaplin and one of the buildings that he frequented along the boardwalk. Chaplin was filming the 1915 movie *By the Sea* when his stunt double disappeared without a trace. The stunt double had worked with Chaplin on a number of previous projects, and the two had formed a strong friendship. Chaplin became so worried about his friend that production of the movie was halted for several days while they searched for the man.

Chaplin's friend had been missing for nearly a week. Chaplin was still worried, but the filming had to continue. Under the pressure of the studio producing the film, another stunt double was hired.

On the seventh day after his friend's disappearance, Chaplin returned to his dressing room with some friends after a long day of filming. The dressing room was in the basement of what is now known as Building 26 on Westminster Avenue. Chaplin and his companions were horrified to find his missing friend dead on the dressing room floor. According to reports, the body was heavily decomposed, soaking wet, and covered in seaweed. Since he had been dead for such a long time, it was impossible for the man to enter Chaplin's dressing room and collapse. Somebody must have brought the corpse to the dressing room and left it for Chaplin to find. Although an investigation was conducted, the mystery remains unsolved nearly one hundred years after it happened.

Building 26 is now an apartment building on the Venice Beach Boardwalk. People who happen to pass by Charlie Chaplin's old basement dressing room can hear strange sounds coming from within. Most frequently, there is a distinct cry for help that will get fainter and fainter until it is replaced by silence. At other times, the sound of splashing water can be heard. It has been described as if somebody is struggling to stay afloat in order to keep from drowning.

Beverly Hills

Beverly Hills Hotel
9641 Sunset Boulevard

The Beverly Hills Hotel was opened to the public on May 12, 1912. It was one of the larger buildings constructed in this area of Beverly Hills. Due to its success, several other businesses were soon built nearby. Some have credited the Beverly Hills Hotel with helping form Beverly Hills as it is seen today.

The Beverly Hills Hotel was used on the album cover of the Eagles's 1976 album *Hotel California*. However, all of the members of the Eagles claim that the song is not about the Beverly Hills Hotel, as some people claim. Today, the Beverly Hills Hotel is positioned on twelve acres in downtown Beverly Hills.

The hotel has twenty-one private bungalows that were frequented by some of the biggest stars of the early twentith century. Unlike hotel rooms, a bungalow is a freestanding structure—a small house with its own separate entrance. Often, the personalities went to the hotel for a bit of privacy from the hustle and bustle of Hollywood life. One of the great benefits of the Beverly Hills Hotel is that the guests' identities remain confidential.

Two of the twenty-one bungalows at the Beverly Hills Hotel are reportedly haunted by at least two former guests. One of the ghosts that is believed to be in a bungalow at the hotel is none other than actor and comedian Harpo Marx.

Harpo Marx of the famous comedy troupe, the Marx Brothers, was quite possibly the most mysterious of the entire group of brothers. In all but one of dozens of movies that the Marx Brothers filmed over their career, he was silent. He developed a unique pantomime routine that caused some to question whether or not Harpo was actually unable to speak. He could speak, and had a very deep, baritone voice that did not match his comedic presence on stage and film. He usually carried a harp that he often used to communicate his emotional reactions, which lead to his friends giving him the nickname Harpo. In the spring of 1964, Harpo Marx officially retired from show business, making his announcement during a public appearance. Within six months of this announcement, Harpo Marx died of a heart attack on September 28, 1964.

If guests of the bungalow that Harpo Marx occasionally stayed at are lucky, they can sometimes hear his telltale harp music playing. Of course, if anybody tries to find out where the harp playing is coming from, they are always unable to find the source.

Ironically, in the Marx Brothers's film *A Day at the Races*, Harpo Marx was seen playing a small portion of Rachmanioff's "Prelude in C# Minor." This is where things get very interesting because the other famous haunting at the Beverly Hills Hotel is none other than Sergei Rachmaninoff himself.

At another bungalow, not far from the one reportedly haunted by Harpo Marx, the famous Russian composer is said to be seen and sometimes heard. Rachmaninoff was born in northern Russia in April 1873. His worldwide fame led him to tour extensively at a breakneck pace in both Europe and the United States. While doing concerts in and near Los Angeles, Rachmanioff was known to stay at the Beverly Hills Hotel as a reprieve from his busy schedule. Rachmaninoff died on March 28, 1943, in Beverly Hills just a few days before his seventieth birthday. After his death, guests of the bungalow where he was known to stay have claimed to have seen his apparition.

Both bungalows are generally booked weeks in advance in order for the guests to have an opportunity to experience the paranormal.

Greystone Mansion/Doheny Mansion
905 Loma Vista Drive

The Greystone Mansion was built in 1928 by oil tycoon Edward Doheny. Shortly after it was completed, Edward Doheny gave the mansion as a gift to his son, Ned Doheny. Ned, his wife Lucy, and their five children moved into the mansion in November 1928. The mansion is nestled among nearly nineteen acres of surrounding property. Today, the mansion and surrounding land is owned by the city of Beverly Hills and is on the National Register of Historic Places. People still use the mansion for weddings and public events such as fund-raisers.

The Greystone Mansion is quite possibly the most recognized mansion in television and film history. Since 1955, the mansion has been used in several high-budget movies including *Flowers in the Attic, There Will Be Blood, X-Men, The Social Network,* and dozens of other major film projects.

Although the mansion is sought after by the entertainment industry and hosts several high-profile events every year, Greystone Mansion has a very dark and deadly past. Just one year after it was constructed, and only four months after Ned and his family moved in, the Greystone Mansion was the scene of two violent deaths that remain unsolved to this day.

During the late-night hours of February 16, 1929, Lucy Doheny woke up to the sound of two gunshots. She went to investigate and found her husband, Ned Doheny, and his personal assistant, Hugh Plunkett, lying dead in the study. She immediately knew that her husband was dead because he had been shot in the head at close range by a .45 caliber revolver. When she looked at Plunkett's body, she noticed that he was still holding the gun that killed them both in his lifeless hand. The official explanation was that Doheny and Plunkett got into a heated argument over finances and that in a fit of rage Plunkett murdered Doheny. Upon realizing what he had done to his longtime associate, Plunkett turned the gun on himself and committed suicide. There has been whispered speculation that there is more to the murder-suicide than meets the eye, including the possibility that both were murdered and the gun was placed in Plunkett's hand after he was dead. There was never any further investigation on the deaths, however.

After the murders, Lucy Doheny did marry again and stayed at the house. It has been said that she never went into the room where she found her husband ever again. Her second husband was rumored to have been in sexual relationships with several of the staff who lived in the mansion. After Lucy Doheny's death, the property was sold and eventually purchased by the city of Beverly Hills.

As usually is the case involving violent deaths, several ghosts have been encountered at the Greystone Mansion.

The first ghost is Lucy Doheny herself. She is usually seen in what used to be her bedroom. An apparition of a woman in her thirties is sometimes seen pacing back and forth in the room, wringing her hands. The smell of a lilac-scented perfume can also be noticed at times. The same apparition has been known to be in the study where Doheny and Plunket violently met their deaths.

Two other ghosts at the mansion are Ned Doheny and Hugh Plunkett. In the study where they both died, people experience a very strong sense of tension and foreboding dread. Although rare, two phantom gunshots can be heard in the room.

The mansion has more ghosts than just the Dohenys and Plunkett. The ghosts of several of the staff have been frequently seen throughout the mansion. A few years after the murder, one of the older maids was in the basement working. While she was in the basement, she felt sharp pains in her chest, had a massive heart attack, and died. When walking through the area of the basement where she died, it has been said that people occasionally experience a sharp pain and shortness of breath. When they leave the area, the feeling subsides.

Another spirit is that of a young maid who had an affair with Lucy Doheny's second husband. The story goes that he had a sexual affair with the maid and she eventually got pregnant. When she approached the husband about the pregnancy, he turned away and refused to help her. In desperation, the maid created a makeshift noose from sheets and hung herself in the doorway in front of the servants' quarters. An apparition of the woman hanging from the doorway can sometimes be seen in this spot.

Pickfair Mansion
1143 Summit Drive

Douglas Fairbanks purchased the hunting lodge and surrounding property for his new wife, Mary Pickford. Pickfair Mansion was named after her. The original Pickfair Mansion reportedly was so elaborate that it took more than five years to complete construction. The four-story structure had over forty rooms to accommodate Douglas Fairbanks's numerous guests, which included such notable figures as Charlie Chaplin, Helen Keller, Sir Arthur Conan Doyle, Thomas Edison, and President Franklin D. Roosevelt and his wife.

The mansion was purchased by actress Pia Zadora in 1988. Originally, the actress said that she was making renovations to the historic building. However, she admitted in 1990 that she had actually demolished the Pickfair Mansion and was building another, more elaborate mansion in its place. The demolition was not initially discovered because of the mansion's secluded location on the property. The demolition of Pickfair Mansion brought harsh criticism from several notable figures from the Hollywood community. However, it appears that the mansion's former resident got his exact revenge for destroying the home that he had loved so much.

After the new, larger mansion was constructed, strange events started to happen. As is commonly known in ghost-hunting investigations, major renovations can often stir up ghostly phenomena. Zadora, her husband, and several staff at the residence have seen the apparition of a man standing at the main entrance. Those who have seen the apparition in detail all agree that the form very closely resembles the original resident of Pickfair Mansion, Douglas Fairbanks. A woman's apparition believed to be Mary Pickford has been seen wandering the property. There have been reports of a strong, almost overwhelming sadness that emanates from both of these spirits.

Santa Monica

....

Santa Monica Municipal Pier

200 Santa Monica Pier, Suite A

The Santa Monica Pier (photo courtesy Library of Congress)

The fabulous Santa Monica Municipal Pier is the final stopping point for our haunted tour of Route 66. It was opened to the public on September 9, 1909, and took over one year to construct. Because of its historic significance, several movies have been filmed on the pier, including *The Sting* and *Funny Girl*.

The Santa Monica Pier has offered a great number of amusement rides, games, and other attractions since it opened in 1909. Some of the more notable rides at the pier over the years have included the Blue Streak Racer and the Whirlwind Dipper roller coasters as well as other activities for people of all ages ... both alive and deceased.

Attached to the pier is one of the Pier's most notable fixtures. The hand-carved, all-wood Santa Monica Carousel has been long-believed to be haunted. It was constructed in 1916 and was used by the public for several years. A tall, shadowy form has been seen riding the carousel horses or walking on the roofs of nearby buildings of the boardwalk since at least 1910.

In the 1950s, the office buildings at Santa Monica Pier were converted into apartments. People who lived in the nearby apartment buildings in the 1960s would also claim to hear people talking outside of their doors at all hours of the night—only to find the hallways empty when they went to investigate. Residents of the apartments who were oblivious to the ghostly reports from the 1910s and 1920s would often see the shadowy person or form walking on the roof of their building or riding the carousel at all hours at night. There have even been claims of people hearing the carousel organ playing in the middle of the night, although the boardwalk was closed and nobody had access to the instrument.

Conclusion

This book has provided a glimpse into the lives of the people and places touched by the supernatural along Route 66. However, these ghost stories are only a small fraction of the hundreds of paranormal encounters that have taken place and continue to take place along the Mother Road. Some of the most interesting and elaborate ghost stories about Route 66 may never reach the printed page. They can be told between friends sitting at a table at a local bar, passed down from father to child while sitting around a campfire, or shared in hushed whispers as friends explore some of the abandoned buildings along Route 66. That is what makes Route 66 such a unique experience…it brings people together in a way that no other roadway in the United States has ever been able to do.

Although the stories in this book (and several stories that may never be shared among the masses) are devoted to the dead and their interactions with the living, this book is really about our connection to each other. The ghosts that have been experienced along Route 66 and in several other locations were once living people who had thoughts, hopes, and fears. They loved. They hated. They entertained. In many cases, they gave the ultimate sacrifice for what they believed in. It doesn't matter if that sacrifice took place several hundred years ago or a few months ago, the ghosts encountered along Route 66 were people.

In my opinion, the abandoned buildings and towns along the Mother Road should be considered hallowed ground and a standing testament to the creativity, ingenuity, and determination of those who came before us. The rusting signs that once glowed with a plethora of neon colors and the buildings where we once lodged, toured, shopped, and dined are a form of memorial that people should gather to and reminisce about a better time in our not-too-distant past.

It has been said that what was old shall become new again. If enough people believe that Route 66 was more than simply 2,448 miles of interconnected asphalt, but rather an entire way of life, then perhaps we can resurrect the spirit of adventure found along Main Street USA and incorporate it into our town, no matter where we are located.

The traveler was active; he went strenuously in search of people, of adventure, of experience. The tourist is passive; he expects interesting things to happen to him. He goes "sight-seeing."
— Daniel J. Boorstin

References

Introduction

Knowles, Drew. *Route 66 Adventure Handbook*. Santa Monica, CA: Santa Monica Press, 2006.

Southall, Richard. *How to Be a Ghost Hunter*. St. Paul, MN: Llewellyn Publications, 2003.

The Great Dictator. Charlie Chaplin. United Artists, 1940.

Illinois

"56 Dead or Missing, 41 Hurt in Elwood Ordnance Blast." *Joliet Herald News*. June 5, 1942: 1.

"Al Capone on Alcatraz." *Al Capone on Alcatraz*. Ocean View Publishing. http://www.alcatrazhistory.com/cap1.htm.

Andreas, A. T. *History of Chicago*, Vol. 2. Chicago: A. T. Andreas, 1885.

"At a Glance, Loyola University Chicago." *Loyola University Chicago*. http://www.luc.edu/keyfacts/index.shtml.

Bachelors Grove Cemetery, The Most Haunted Place in the World. Bachelor's Grove Paranormal Forums. http://www.bachelors-grove.com.

Bergreen, Laurence. *Capone the Man and the Era*. New York: Simon & Schuster, 1994.

Bonansinga, Jay R. *The Sinking of the Eastland: America's Forgotten Tragedy*. New York: Citadel, 2004.

"Brief History of the Red Lion Pub." *The Red Lion Pub—Home Page*. http://www.redlionchicago.com/history.html.

"Chicago's Haunted Red Lion Pub." http://occultview.com/2009/03/03/chicagos-haunted-red-lion-pub/

"Clarendon Hills Country House Ghost Story." *Clarendon Hills Country House*. http://www.burgerone.com/clarendon/ghost-story.html.

Clearfield, Dylan. "Dillinger's Ghost." *HubPages*. August 5, 2011. http://dylanclearfield.hubpages.com/hub/Dillingers-Ghost.

Cromie, Robert. *The Great Chicago Fire*. New York: Rutledge Hill, 1994.

"Dillinger Slain in Chicago; Shot Dead by Federal Men in Front of Movie Theatre." *The New York Times*. July 22, 1934: 1.

Eastland Memorial Society. http://www.eastlandmemorial.org.

"Famous Cases and Criminals: John Dillinger." *Famous Cases and Criminals*. Federal Bureau of Investigation. http://www.fbi.gov/about-us/history/famous-cases/john-dillinger/

"F.S. Allen—Architect." *Joliet—Community Web Site for the City of Joliet*. http://www.cityofjoliet.com/halloffame/artists/fsallen.htm.

Gorner, Peter. "Some of Chicago's Favorite Haunts." *Chicago Tribune*. May 13, 1974, sec. B: 13.

Hauck, William. *Haunted Places, The National Directory*. New York: Penguin Books, 1996.

"Haunted Chicago Locations Page 1." *Haunted Chicago Paranormal Research and Investigation*. http://www.hauntedchicago.com/location1.htm.

"Haunted Illinois from H to L." http://www.angelfire.com/scary/chicago haunts/page3.htm.

"Haunted Places in Illinois—Will County Ghost Hunters Society." *Will County Ghost Hunters Society*. http://www.aghostpage.com/haunted-placesinillinois.htm.

"The Haunted Harpo Studios." *You Got GHOSTS, Girl!!* http://song-birdsisters.tripod.com/harpo.html.

"Haunt in Frank Shaver Allen House, Corner of Morgan and Dewey Streets Joliet, Il 60433 Joliet, Illinois, Will Haunt." http://www.strangeusa .com/Viewlocation.aspx?id=2978.

"The Hauntings of Harpo Studios." *Chicago Unbelievable*. May 20, 2011. http://www.chicagounbelievable.com/2011/05/hauntings-of-harpo-studios.html.

Helmer, William J., and Arthur J. Bilek. *The St. Valentine's Day Massacre: the Untold Story of the Gangland Bloodbath That Brought Down Al Capone*. Nashville, TN: Cumberland House, 2006.

Hilton, George W. *Eastland: Legacy of the Titanic*. Stanford, CA: Stanford University Press, 1996.

"History—Graceland Cemetery." *Graceland Cemetery, Chicago IL*. http://www.gracelandcemetery.org/pages/history.html.

"History." *Rialto Square Theatre*. http://www.rialtosquare.com/history.asp.

Hucke, Matthew. "Mount Carmel Catholic Cemetery." 1997. http:// graveyards.com/IL/Cook/mtcarmel.

"Hull House Ghost Pictures." *Hull House Ghost Pictures*. Chicago Unbelievable, March 10, 2011. http://www.chicagounbelievable.com/2011/03/hull-house-ghost-pictures.html.

"Hunting a Ghost Named Mary." *Chicago Tribune*. October 31, 1985.

"The Inn at 835." *Ghost Haunters*. http://www.ghosthaunters.com/index.php?pr=The_Inn_At_835.

"Investigations." *Springfield Ghost Society*. April 30, 2003. http://springfieldghostsociety.com/sgs/Investigations/StGeorgeHotel/StGeorgeHotelHistory.html.

JADA—Joliet Arsenal Development. http://jada.org/history.htm.

Johnson, Mary A. "Hull House." *Encyclopedia of Chicago*. Chicago Historical Society, 2005. http://www.encyclopedia.chicagohistory.org/pages/615.html.

"Killed in Crash." *Chicago Tribune*. March 12, 1934: 5.

Matera, Dary. *John Dillinger: The Life and Death of America's First Celebrity Criminal*. New York: Carroll & Graf, 2004.

"Mount Carmel Cemetery." *Ghost Research Society*. http://www.ghostresearch.org/sites/carmel.html.

Oetzel, Shawn. "Wrigley Field: The Haunted Confines?" *Associatedcontent.com*. September 1, 2010. http://www.associatedcontent.com/article/5723228/wrigley_field_the_haunted_confines_pg2.html?cat=14.

"'The Oprah Winfrey Show': Trivia—Oprah.com." *Oprah Winfrey's Official Website—Live Your Best Life—Oprah.com*. http://www.oprah.com/oprahshow/The-Oprah-Winfrey-Show-Trivia.

Pierce, Bessie L. *A History of Chicago: Volume III: The Rise of a Modern City, 1871–1893*. Vol. III. Chicago: University of Chicago, 1957, Rep. 2007.

Purvis, Alston W., and Alex Tresinowski. *The Vendetta: FBI Hero Melvin Purvis's War against Crime, and J. Edgar Hoover's War against Him.* New York: Public Affairs, 2005.

Raab, Selwyn. *Five Families: The Rise, Decline, and Resurgence of America's Most Powerful Mafia Empires.* New York: Thomas Dunne Books, 2005.

"Resurrection Catholic Cemetery: Resurrection Mary." *Graveyards. com—Graveyards of Illinois—Graveyards of Chicago.* http://graveyards .com/IL/Cook/resurrection/mary.html.

Riess, Steven A. *Touching Base: Professional Baseball and American Culture in the Progressive Era.* Urbana, IL: University of Illinois, 1999.

Robson, Ellen, and Dianne Halicki. *Haunted Highway: The Spirits of Route 66.* Phoenix, AZ: Golden West, 2008.

"Rosehill Cemetery." *Clarendon Hills Country House.* http://www.burger one.com/clarendon/ghost-story.html.

"Rosehill Cemetery." *Halloween and Horror at HorrorSeek.com—HorrorHost.com.* April 13, 2007. http://usersites.horrorfind.com/home/ ghosts/hauntedus/rosehill.htm.

Saunders, Rhys. "Dana-Thomas House' Creepy Tales Revealed." *The State Journal-Register.* (Springfield, IL) October 25, 2009. http://www.sj-r.com/ x884486934/Guide-tells-creepy-tales-about-Dana-Thomas-House- during-nighttime-tour.

Springfield Theatre Centre—Springfield, IL Home. http://www.spring fieldtheatrecentre.com.

"Springfield—The Indiana Paranormal Society." *Active Message Board List—Aimoo.* March 3, 2009. http://forum3.aimoo.com/IndianaParanormal Society/Illinois/Springfield-1-401740.html.

"The O'Leary Legend." *Chicago History Museum.* Chicago History Museum, October 1, 1997.

"The Saint Valentine's Day Massacre—HauntedHouses.com." *Haunted Houses & Halloween*. Video Producers, Inc. August 5, 2011. http://www.hauntedhouses.com/states/il/saint_valentines_day_massacre.htm.

Uittenbogaard, Arie. "The Biograph Theater." *Ghost Stories and Haunted Places*. March 24, 2010. http://ghoststoriesandhauntedplaces.blogspot.com/2010/03/biograph-theater.html.

Uittenbogaard, Arie. "The Chicago Water Tower That Survived the Fire." *The Chicago Water Tower That Survived the Fire*. October 8, 2010. http://ghoststoriesandhauntedplaces.blogspot.com/2010/10/water-tower.html.

Wachholz, Ted. *The Eastland Disaster*. Charleston, SC: Arcadia, 2005.

Welcome to the Dana-Thomas House. August 7, 2011. http://www.dana-thomas.org.

Wood, Robert M. *Did Biela's Comet Cause the Chicago and Midwest Fires?* 2004 Planetary Defense Conference: Protecting Earth from Asteroids, Orange County, California. *2004 Planetary Defense Conference: Protecting Earth from Asteroids*. American Institute of Aeronautics and Astronautics. February 26, 2004. http://pdf.aiaa.org/preview/CDReadyMPDC04_865/PV2004_1419.pdf.

"Wrigley Field." *ballparks.com*. N.p., May 2008. http://www.ballparks.com/baseball/national/wrigle.htm.

Missouri

"Bissell Mansion Restaurant & Murder Mystery Theatre." http://www.bissellmansiontheatre.com/History.htm.

"City of Bridgeton: Payne-Gentry House." http://www.bridgetonmo.com/DesktopDefault.aspx?tabid=60.

Elbin, Jennifer. "Peace Church Cemetery and the Ghost of Joplin, Missouri." April 13, 2008. http://www.associatedcontent.com/article/701287/peace_church_cemetery_and_the_ghost.html?cat=37.

"Find a grave: Lewis Bissell (1789-1868)." http://www.findagrave.com/cgi-bin/fg.cgi?page=gr&GRid=18501.

"Ghosts and Haunts in Missouri: Doling Cave Stories." 2007. http://www.missourighosts.net/dolingcavestories.html.

"Ghosts and Haunts in Missouri: Freudenberger Ghost Stories." 2007. http://www.missourighosts.net/freudenbergerstories.html.

Goodwin, Dave. "Camp Leonard Wood: The Righteous Ghosts of Bloodland." 2003. http://www.militaryghosts.com/l_wood.html.

"Guide to the Archival Collections at the Missouri Historical Society." http://www.krausehouse.ca/Krause/Archives%20Guide%20A-Z%20(WP).htm.

Hacker, John and David Hoover. "Not quite haunted, but … Paranormal investigators look into spirit activity at Kendrick House. Carthage Press (Missouri)." November 17, 2008.

"Haunted Missouri Directory." August 28, 2009. http://hauntedmo.110mb.com/stl.html.

"Haunted Places in Missouri." http://theshadowlands.net/places/missouri.htm.

"Landers Theater History." 2011. http://www.springfieldlittletheatre.org/about/history/landers-theatre-history/

"Missouri Legends: Haunted Bissell Mansion in St. Louis." 2011. http://www.legendsofamerica.com/mo-bissellmansion.html.

"Missouri Paranormal Experience: Haunted Springfield." 2010. http://paranormalexperience.wetpaint.com/page/Haunted%20Springfield?t=anon.

"Paranormal Science Lab: Kendrick Place Historical Civil War House." 2010. http://paranormalsciencelab.com/kendrick.html.

"Paranormal Task Force: Zombie Road History and Haunting Mini-Site." 2011. http://www.paranormaltaskforce.com/ZombieRoad.html.

"Springfield Hauntings: Landers Theater." 2006. September 15, 2011. www
.hauntedhouses.com/states/mo/landers_theater.htm.

"The Lemp Mansion Restaurant and Inn." 2011. http://www.lemp
mansion.com/

"Trivia: Ghosts: Lemp Mansion." 2010. http://www.funtrivia.com/en/
subtopics/The-Lemp-Mansion-299890.html.

Vandergriff, Jim. "The Legend of Joe's Cave: Murder, Medicine, Counter-
feiting, and Vigilantism." MFS Journal 15-16 (1994): 29-50.

Kansas

"The Eldridge Ghost." *The Eldridge Hotel—Lawrence Kansas Historic Hotel.*
Web. 18 Feb. 2012. http://www.eldridgehotel.com.

Fitzgerald, Daniel C. "Kansas Ghost Towns: The Top Ten." *The Best of Everything in Kansas.* Daniel C Fitzgerald. http://www.danielcfitzgerald.com/
top10kansasghosttowns.html.

McKinney, Roger. "Ghost Hunters to Investigate Two Galen Graveyards."
The Joplin (Missouri) *Globe.* February 21, 2007. http:/www.joplin
globe.com/local/x212047714/Ghost-hunters-to-investigate-two-
Galena-graveyards.

"Mrs. Amantha Hatch Set The Time of Her Death. Husband Received
Warning." *Kansas City Journal.* November 22, 1907.

"A Murderous Tale of Scandal, and Treasure in Galena, Kansas." *Legends
of America—American History, People, Legends, Old West, Travel Destinations, and Lots More. For the Nostaligic and Historic Minded.* http://
www.legendsofamerica.com/ks-galenatreasure.html.

Stokes, Keith. "Route 66 in Kansas (Galena)." *Kansas Travel, Tourism &
Restaurants.* http://www.kansastravel.org/route66.htm.

Young, Foster. *The Ozark Spook Light.* 1881.

Wood, Larry. "Jesse James' Death Hoax and Buried Treasure." *Jesse James' Death Hoax and Buried Treasures*. http://www.jessejamesintexas.com/letters.htm.

Oklahoma

B., Amy. "Our Visit to the Haunted Coleman Theater at Miami, Oklahoma." *Yahoo! Voices—Voices.yahoo.com*. 3 Sept. 2009. http://voices.yahoo.com/part-2-our-visit-haunted-coleman-theater-at-4191399.html?cat=16.

"Belvidere Mansion." *Belvidere Mansion*. August 18, 2007. http://www.okpri.com/BelvidereMansion.htm.

"Bryant Center Revisited." *Abandoned Oklahoma*. http://www.abandonedok.com/bryant-center-revisited/

Current Tulsa Hunts. Paranormal Investigation Team of Tulsa (PITT) Ghost and Haunting Research Professionals, 2011. http://www.pittok.com/haunted_tulsa/

Driftglass. "Tulsa County." *Haunted Oklahoma: Haunted Legends of the Sooner State*. May 27, 2009. http://hauntedoklahoma.blogspot.com/2009/05/tulsa-county.html.

"The Ghost Still Walks! Ella Myers Haunts Those Who Injured Her. Is Her Body Upside Down?" *Guthrie Daily Leader*. April 19, 1896.

Hirsch, James S. *Riot and Remembrance: the Tulsa Race War and Its Legacy*. Boston: Houghton Mifflin, 2002.

Lunsford, Rhonda. "Tulsa Garden Center History." *Paranormal Investigation Team of Tulsa*. http://members.tripod.com/okpitt/id78.html.

Mattingly-Arthur, Megan. "Haunted Houses by Claremore, Oklahoma." Travel Tips—*USAToday.com*. December 22, 2011. http://traveltips.usatoday.com/haunted-houses-claremore-oklahoma-62247.html.

"No Inquest Needed. Ella Myers Associates Were The Cause of Her Hasty Burial!" *Guthrie Daily Leader*. April 9, 1896: 8.

"No More Ghost! The Remains of Ella Myers Exhumed And Found Right Side Up!" *Guthrie Daily Leader*. April 23, 1896: 4.

Plain, Terri. "Ghosts Pictures & Stories." *Official Website Of P.P.I. Paranormal Investigations. P.P.I. Paranormal*, 2011. http://www.freewebs .com/ghosts4/hauntings.htm.

"Real Ghost Stories from Oklahoma." *Real Ghost Stories from Oklahoma*. http://ghouli2.tripod.com/reportsvideoandmisc/id7.html.

"Red Hand Appeared. House In Which a Cyprian Died, Said to Be Haunted!" *Guthrie Daily Leader*. April 15, 1896: 4.

Sutton, Roseanne. "The Constantine Theater—Is It Haunted?" *Pawhuska Journal Capital* (Oklahoma). October 20, 2010. http://www.pawhuska journalcapital.com/articles/2010/10/20/lifestyles/life01.txt.

"Tulsa Garden Center Mansion History." *Tulsa Garden Center Information*. http://www.tulsagardencenter.com/htdocs/TGCMansion/ TGChistory.htm.

"Tulsa Tuesday— Haunted Places in Tulsa | The Lost Ogle." *The Lost Ogle—Oklahoma City, Oklahoma*. October 28, 2008. http://www .thelostogle.com/2008/10/28/tulsa-tuesday-haunted-places-in-tulsa/

Weiser, Kathy. "The Haunted Belvidere Mansion in Claremore, Oklahoma." *Legends of America*, January 2009. http://www.legendsofamerica.com/ ok-belvideremansion.html.

Texas

Allen, Donna. "Ghost Hunting 101: Where Can I Hunt for Ghosts in Fort Worth?" August 11, 2009. http://www.examiner.com/ghost-hunting-in-dallas/ghost-hunting-101-where-can-i-hunt-for-ghosts-fort-worth.

Beck, Wayne E. "The Phantom Killer of Texarkana." *The Phantom Killer of Texarkana*. December 9, 2010. http://www.txkphantom.site11.com/index2.html.

Balsiger, David W., and Charles E. Sellier. *The Lincoln Conspiracy*. Los Angeles, CA: Schick Sunn Classic, 1977.

"Catfish Plantation—Paranormal Activity." *Catfish Plantation—Serving Soul and Spirits!* http://www.catfishplantation.com/paranormal index.html.

"Catfish Plantation." *Hauntedhouses.com*. http://www.hauntedhouses.com/states/tx/catfish_plantation.htm.

"Fort Concho." *Military Ghosts—Haunted Forts, Posts & Battlefields*. http://www.militaryghosts.com/concho.html.

"Ghost Hunt of Fort Richardson, Texas." *Fort Richardson Investigation Report*. Southwest Ghost Hunters Association, 2005. http://www.sgha.net/tx/jacksboro/ftr.html.

"Ghost Stories of Log Cabin Village." http://www.logcabinvillage.org/docments/ghost_stories.pdf.

"Ghosts of Fort Concho." Ghosts Wiki. http://ghosts.wikia.com/wiki/Fort_Concho.

"Ghosttraveller: Big Ass Texas Ghosts." *Ghosttraveller: Collected Ghost Stories and Other Disturbing Americana*. http://www.ghosttraveller.com/Texas.htm.

Gold, Yona. "Haunted Places in Dallas, TX." *Yahoo! Voices—Voices.yahoo.com*. 2011. http://voices.yahoo.com/haunted-places-dallas-tx-1037031.html?cat=16.

"Granbury, TX—Official Website—John Wilkes Booth." *Granbury, TX—Official Website*. http://www.granbury.org/index.aspx?NID=705.

Hamilton, Allen L. "Fort Richardson: The Handbook of Texas Online." *A Digital Gateway to Texas History.* Texas State Historical Association (TSHA). http://www.tshaonline.org/handbook/online/articles/qbf41.

Hopkins, Bob. "Ghosts of the Baker Hotel, Mineral Wells, Texas: All about Texas—Texas Travel, History, Attractions, over 2,700 Cities, Towns, Ghost Towns; People, Historic Places, Buildings, Illustrated." *Texas Escapes Online Magazine.* March 21, 2009. http://www.texasescapes.com/Texas-PanhandleTowns/MineralWellsTexas/BakerHotelGhosts.htm.

"The Humpback Haunting of Oklahoma's Route 66." *Strange State: Paranormal Mysteries & More.* http://strangestate.blogspot.com/2010/04/legend-has-it-that-along-route-66.html.

"IPI—Amarillo, TX." *Indiana Paranormal Ghosts, Demons, History and Haunted Houses.* http://www.indianaparanormal.com/amarillo.html.

"Jacksboro." *Jack County—Jacksboro, Texas.* Jacksboro Chamber of Commerce, 1999. http://www.jacksboro-tx.com/areainfo.html.

"The Lady of the Log Cabin Village . . . and Other Spirited Tales from Cowtown's Crypt." *Fort Worth Star-Telegram* October 31, 2004, Sunday Life Section.

Newton, Michael. *The Encyclopedia of Serial Killers.* New York: Facts on File, 2006.

"Outlaw Relocation Program, Granbury, Texas." *Roadside America—Guide to Uniquely Odd Tourist Attractions.* http://www.roadside america.com/story/2223.

Righi, Brian. *Ghosts of Fort Worth: Investigating Cowtown's Most Haunted Locations.* Atglen, PA: Schiffer Publishing, 2007.

"River Legacy Park—Hells Gate." *Hauntings Paranormal Social Network.* Shipp Enterprises, LLC, 2011. http://hauntin.gs/Texas/Arlington/River%20Legacy%20Park-%20Hells%20Gate/1126//.

"San Antonio Ghost Hunters." *San Antonio Paranormal Network*, 2011. http://www.ghost411.com/texas_hauntings.

"A Step-by-Step Encounter of Another Kind." *Fort Worth Star-Telegram,* October 31, 1992, Life Sec.

Swanson, James L. *Manhunt: The 12-Day Chase for Lincoln's Killer.* New York: HarperCollins, 2006.

"Texas GenDisasters...Genealogy in Tragedy, Disasters, Fires, Floods." *GenDisasters: Events That Touched Our Ancestors' Lives.* http://www3 .gendisasters.com/taxonomy_menu/2/43?page=2http://ghostand-souls.wordpress.com/.

"Texas Town List, over 2,800 Texas Small Towns, Cities, Towns and Ghost Towns." December 1, 2011. http://www.texasescapes.com/TOWNS/ Texas_towns_A_to_Z.htm.

Weiser, Kathy. "Alton, Texas and Goatman's Bridge." *Legends of America.* July 2010. http://www.legendsofamerica.com/tx-alton.html.

Williams, Yona. "Haunted Colleges in the United States." *Unexplainable.Net—UFOS, Ghosts, Paranormal, 2012 And More—Latest News.* Unexplainable.net,July8,2010.http://www.unexplainable.net/Ghost-Paranormal/Haunted-Colleges-in-the-United-States.shtml.

New Mexico

Beitler, Stu. "Madrid, NM Coal Mine Explosion, Dec 1932." *GenDisasters: Events that Touched Our Ancestors' Lives.* http://www3.gendisasters .com/new-mexico/5993/madrid-nm-coal-mine-explosion-dec-1932.

"La Posada Hotel." *Unsolved Mysteries Wiki.* http://unsolvedmysteries .wikia.com/wiki/La_Posada_Hotel.

"Maria Teresa Restaurant." *New Mexico Tourism Department.* http:// www.newmexico.travel/dev/western/experience/maria_teresa.php.

Morehouse, George E. "The Los Lunas Inscriptions, a Geological Study," Epigraphic Society, Occasional Publications, 13:44, 1985.

"The Mystery of the Miracle Bell—Unexplained—IN SEARCH FOR TRUTH." *In Search for the Truth*. http://istina.rin.ru/eng/ufo/text/ 183.html.

Nathanson, Rick. "Is the KiMo Theatre Really Haunted by the Spirit of a Boy Killed There in 1951, or Is It Urban Legend?" *Albuquerque Journal*, August 2, 2009, Final ed., E-1. http://www.abqjournal.com/lifestyles /0221357lifestyles08-02-09.htm.

Neuhoff, Juergen. "Los Lunas Decalogue—Introduction." *Los Lunas Decalogue*. October 17, 2007. http://www.mhccorp.com/archaeology /decalogue-introduction.html.

"The Oldest House in America." *The Oldest House in America: Santa Fe's Casa Vieja de Analco*. http://chuck.hubpages.com/hub/The-Oldest-House-in-America.

"The Place of Scary—Haunted Places." *The Place Of Scary—Haunted Places*. November 2009. http://hauntedplacesofusa.blogspot.com/ 2009_11_01_archive.html.

Robson, Ellen, and Dianne Halicki. *Haunted Highway: the Spirits of Route 66*. Phoenix, AZ: Golden West, 2008.

"The San Jose Bell." *Ashley Fetner Fine Art Photography*. http://www .ashleyfetnerportraits.com/blog/?p=1340.

"Shadowlands Haunted Places Index—New Mexico." *The Shadowlands*. http://www.theshadowlands.net/places/newmexico.htm.

Weiser, Kathy. "The Ghosts of Albuquerque, New Mexico." *Legends of America—A Travel Site for the Nostalgic and Historic Minded*. http:// www.legendsofamerica.com/nm-albuquerqueghosts.html.

"Welcome to Historic Mission San Miguel." *Mission San Miguel*. http:// www.missionsanmiguel.com.

Weiser, Kathy. "Madrid—A Ghost Town Reborn." *Legends of America.* http://www.legendsofamerica.com/nm-madrid.html.

Arizona

"A&B Schuster Co. Collection, 1862–1952." *Arizona Archives Online.* http://www.azarchivesonline.org.

"Arizona's Haunted Hotspots." *Carpe Noctem—Seize the Night.* http://www.carpenoctem.tv/haunted-hotspots/arizona/

"Arizona Road Segments—Route 66: A Discover Our Shared Heritage Travel Itinerary." *U.S. National Park Service—Experience Your America.* http://www.nps.gov/nr/travel/route66/arizona_road_segments.html.

Branning, Debe. "Ghosts of the Riordan Mansion—Phoenix Arizona Haunted Sites." *Examiner.com.* June 13, 2009. http:/www.examiner.com/arizona-haunted-sites-in-phoenix/ghosts-of-the-riordan-mansion.

———"Teen Angel Ghost of Comfi Cottages in Flagstaff Arizona—Phoenix Arizona Haunted Sites." *Examiner.com.* January 15, 2010. http://www.examiner.com/arizona-haunted-sites-in-phoenix/teen-angel-ghost-of-comfi-cottages-flagstaff-arizona.

"Comfi Cottages of Flagstaff—A Bed and Breakfast in Flagstaff, Arizona." http://www.theinnkeeper.com/bnb/3190.

"Dark Haunts Arizona Story Index." *Dark Haunts Home Page.* http://darkhaunts.com/ArizonaGhostStoryIndex.html.

"Flagstaff Landmark Since 1931." *World Famous Museum Club.* http://themuseumclub.com/

"A Flagstaff Weekend." *Phoenix Is Haute.* http://phoenixishaute.blogspot.com/2011/05/flagstaff-adventure.html.

"Ghost Hunt of The Inn at Jerome, Jerome, AZ." *Southwest Ghost Hunters Association.* http://www.sgha.net/az/jerome/innatjerome.html.

"Ghosttraveller: Arizona." *Ghosttraveller: Collected Ghost Stories and OtherDisturbingAmericana*.http://www.ghosttraveller.com/arizona.htm.

"Haunted Arizona." *Southwest Ghost Hunters Association*. 2008. http://www.sgha.net/az/invest_az.html.

"Haunted Monte Vista Hotel in Flagstaff Arizona." *Legends of America—American History, People, Legends, Old West, Travel Destinations, and Lots More For the Nostaligic and Historic Minded*. http://www.legend-sofamerica.com/az-montevista.html.

"The Historic Hotel Monte Vista Is Haunted: Phontom Bellboys and Bank Robbers, Servants and Dancers Have All Made the Monte Vista Their Permanent Home." *The Hotel Monte Vista: Flagstaff Arizona's Premier Historic Hotel*. http://www.hotelmontevista.com/hauntedhotel.php.

"A History of the Vulture Gold Mine in Arizona." *About the Vulture Gold Mine*. http://www.jpc-training.com/vulture.htm.

"Hotel Brunswick (Historical), Kingman Arizona Haunted Ghost Hotel." http://www.allstays.com/Haunted/az_kingman_hotelbrunswick.htm.

Houk, Rose. "Arizona State Parks: Riordan Mansion: Home." *Arizona State Parks: Riordan Mansion State Park*. http://azstateparks.com/Parks/RIMA/index.html.

"Jerome Grand Hotel; Arizona Lodging Accommodations near Sedona." http://www.jeromegrandhotel.net.

"Jerome Mile High Inn and Grill, Lodging in Jerome, AZ." http://www.innatjerome.com.

"London Bridge Ghost Tours." http://www.sirgothic.com/Thetour.html.

Mathis, Gay. "An Arizona Hanging—George Smiley—Frank Wattron—Sheriff of Navajo County." True West Historical Society—Official Site of True West Magazine, Since 1953. *True West*, September 8, 2010. http://truewest.ning.com/profiles/blogs/an-arizona-hanginggeorge.

"Oatman-Gold Road Chamber of Commerce in Oatman Arizona on Historical Route 66." October 10, 2011. http://www.oatmangoldroad.org.

"Vacation Cottages Arizona. Family Lodging." http://www.comficottages.com/919_beaver.htm.

"Welcome to GoTourAZ." http://www.gotouraz.com/holbrook2.html.

California

"Calico California—Revived From A Desert Grave." *Legends of America—American History, People, Legends, Old West, Travel Destinations, and Lots More. For the Nostaligic and Historic Minded.* http://www.legendsofamerica.com/ca-calico.html.

"Calico Ghost Town."http://cms.sbcounty.gov/parks/Parks/CalicoGhost Town.aspx.

Cook, Bill. "Calico Ghost Walk Is a Walk You Will Never Forget." *Calico Ghost Walk.* http://www.calicoghostwalk.com.

"Haunt in Pickfair Mansion." *Welcome to Strangeusa.com!* http://www.strangeusa.com/Viewlocation.aspx?id=274.

"Haunted Places in California." *The Shadowlands.* February 2010. http://theshadowlands.net/places/california1.htm.

"Mystery of The Greystone Mansion Murders." *New York Social Diary.* August 30, 2007. http://www.newyorksocialdiary.com/node/2550.

Robson, Ellen, and Dianne Halicki. *Haunted Highway: the Spirits of Route 66.* Phoenix, AZ: Golden West, 2008.

Senate, Richard. "Ghosts Stalk the Greystone Mansion." *Haunted America Tours.* May 6, 2007. http://www.hauntedamericatours.com/ghoststories/GreystoneMansion/

Weeks, John. "The Inland Empire's Best Ghost Stories." *San Bernardino County Sun.* October 29, 2009. http://www.sbsun.com/news/ci_ 13670580.

Weiser, Kathy. "Suicide Bridge in Pasadena, California." *Legends of America—American History, People, Legends, Old West, Travel Destinations, and Lots More for the Nostaligic and Historic Minded.* February 2010. http://www.legendsofamerica.com/ca-suicidebridge.html.

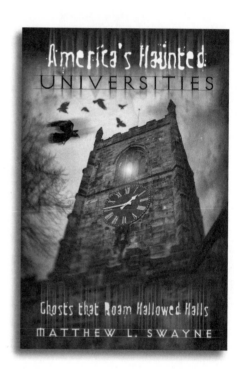